THE BUSY ADULT DECLUTTERING BLUEPRINT

Practical Steps to Organize Your Space and Life

TABLE OF CONTENTS

INTRODUCTION

RECLAIMING CLARITY AMIDST THE CHAOS

As the sun stretched its gentle rays through my office window one morning, it illuminated a scene of chaos that had become an all-too-familiar backdrop to my daily life. My desk, once a pristine surface for creativity and productivity, was now buried beneath a haphazard collection of paperwork—bills, reports, and long-forgotten to-do lists mingling with the remnants of hurried meals. Coffee stains, like dark constellations, marked the trajectory of countless late nights, while sticky notes, those colorful beacons of good intentions, fluttered from every surface, their messages long since faded from memory. My once-trusty laptop, the gateway to my professional world, lay entombed beneath a jumble of stray snacks, tangled charging cables, and miscellaneous office supplies, a monument to my dwindling control over my environment.

This wasn't just a messy desk; it was a mirror reflecting the internal disarray that had slowly crept into my life. The relentless demands of my career, the constant barrage of emails, and the ever-present pressure to "do it all" had gradually eroded my sense of order and left me feeling overwhelmed and adrift. That morning, as I surveyed the wreckage of my workspace, a wave of weariness washed over me. It was a tipping point, a stark and undeniable reminder of how profoundly disorganized my life had become amidst the relentless whirlwind of professional obligations. In that moment of stark clarity, a flicker of resolve ignited within me—a determination to reclaim not just my physical workspace, but also my mental clarity, my sense of purpose, and the elusive peace that had become a distant memory.

For countless busy professionals, individuals juggling demanding careers, family responsibilities, and the ever-increasing pressures of modern life, the challenge of balancing professional ambitions with the desire for an orderly and serene home environment often feels like an insurmountable obstacle.

The very notion of maintaining a sense of control and equilibrium during a relentless schedule seems, at best, a distant dream, and at worst, an impossible aspiration.

Imagine, if you will, stepping into your workspace each morning, whether it's a dedicated home office or a corner of your living room, only to be greeted by a scene of disarray that mirrors the overwhelming demands of your schedule. Piles of unopened mail teeter precariously on surfaces, stacks of unread documents threaten to topple over, and the general sense of disorder creates an immediate feeling of stress and anxiety. The irony is palpable, almost mocking: our material clutter, the physical manifestation of our disorganization, so often serves as a powerful and tangible reflection of the internal chaos that we struggle to contain within ourselves.

Yet, positing order and organization is about far more than mere aesthetics or superficial outward appearances. It transcends the desire for a visually pleasing environment and delves into the fundamental aspects of enhancing the very quality of our lives.

A well-organized environment, whether it's our home or our workspace, acts as a powerful catalyst for increased productivity, fostering a sense of focus and allowing us to approach tasks with greater efficiency and clarity. It plays a crucial role in reducing stress levels, creating a sense of calm and tranquility that counteracts the pressures of daily life. Ultimately, it contributes significantly to improved overall well-being, providing a foundation for greater mental clarity, emotional stability, and a renewed sense of purpose. Transforming a cluttered and chaotic space into one that inspires efficiency, promotes creativity, and fosters a sense of calm can revolutionize the way we approach our daily tasks, both professionally and personally.

In the ever-accelerating pace of modern life, where the boundaries between work and home have become increasingly blurred, particularly for those embracing the flexibility of working from home, maintaining a productive and organized environment is no longer a luxury it's an absolute necessity.

The rise of remote work has brought with it many benefits, including greater autonomy and flexibility, but it has also presented new challenges, such as the potential for distractions, the difficulty of separating work life from personal life, and the risk of burnout. In this context, the ability to create and maintain a clutter-free and organized workspace becomes even more critical for success and well-being.

However, despite the clear benefits of a clutter-free environment, many individuals view decluttering as an overwhelming and daunting task, one that requires an enormous investment of time and energy, often involving the sacrifice of entire weekends dedicated solely to the arduous tasks of sorting, organizing, and discarding possessions. This misconception is widespread, and understandably so. The prospect of facing down years of accumulated belongings, of making hard decisions about what to keep and what to let go, can be paralyzing. But what if I told you that transforming your space, and by extension, transforming your life, doesn't cause enormous time commitments or Herculean efforts?

What if I could offer you a path to order and tranquility that doesn't involve sacrificing your precious weekends or enduring hours of overwhelming labor? What if I told you that the key to lasting change lies in the power of small, consistent actions, and that just fifteen minutes a day, a mere sliver of your busy schedule, could be the catalyst for a profound rejuvenation of your surroundings, making them feel lighter, more inviting, and infinitely more conducive to creativity, productivity, and peace?

The beauty of decluttering lies not in grand, sweeping gestures, but in the subtle yet powerful simplicity of small, habitual steps. Recognize that true and lasting transformation rarely comes from drastic measures; instead, it comes from consistently applying small, manageable actions that gradually accumulate into significant and sustainable results.

The key, then, lies in cultivating consistency, in embracing the understanding that even the most modest efforts, when repeated regularly, have the potential to compound over time, leading to profound and transformative change.

Consider this: by dedicating just a few moments each day to systematically streamline your environment, to tackle one small area, one drawer, or one pile of papers at a time, you progressively create a space that not only effectively supports your professional ambitions and enhances your productivity but also nurtures your personal growth, fosters a sense of calm, and contributes to your overall well-being.

This book unravels the pervasive myths and misconceptions that often shroud decluttering, presenting it not as an insurmountable chore, but as an empowering and achievable journey. It aims to illustrate, with clarity and practicality, how manageable and adaptable decluttering can truly be, regardless of the unique challenges and constraints of your individual circumstances. With the right strategies, the right mindset, and the right approach, integrating decluttering into your daily routine becomes not only possible but also a seamless and natural part of your life, regardless of the intensity and demands of your career or the complexities of your personal responsibilities.

We specifically designed the solutions and techniques in this book to resonate with your fast-paced and demanding lifestyle. They are pragmatic, actionable, and carefully tailored to fit seamlessly into your existing routine without requiring a complete and overhaul of your habits or a radical restructuring of your schedule.

Picture, for a moment, the remarkable sense of accomplishment and empowerment that will gradually unfold as, little by little, step by step, you conquer the clutter that has silently and insidiously drained your time, your energy, and your sense of well-being. Imagine the feeling of lightness and freedom as you shed the burden of unnecessary possessions and create a space that breathes and flows with ease. Envision the clarity of mind and the renewed sense of focus that will emerge as you eliminate the visual and mental distractions that have been holding you back.

By the end of a month, or perhaps even sooner, these small victories, these consistent acts of decluttering, will coalesce to transform not just your physical space, but also your outlook on life, your approach to challenges, and your overall sense of well-being.

The chaos that once prevailed, the feeling of being overwhelmed and out of control, will gradually give way to a sense of reclaimed time, a restored sense of tranquility, and a renewed feeling of empowerment.

Think of decluttering as far more than a mundane household chore or a tedious task to be endured. See it instead as a powerful and transformative investment in your overall well-being, a strategic tool for enhancing your career success, and a pathway to creating a life that is both more productive and more fulfilling. A streamlined and organized environment fosters a mindset that is ready and equipped to meet challenges with vitality, creativity, and unwavering vigor. It provides a solid foundation for success in all areas of life, allowing you to approach your work with greater focus and efficiency, while also creating a sanctuary of peace and tranquility in your personal life.

As you embark on this transformative journey, let this book serve as your trusted guide, your constant companion, offering practical tips, proven systems, and inspiring anecdotes gleaned from the experiences of countless individuals who have walked similar paths and successfully navigated the challenges of decluttering during busy lives. We will explore together the art of perfectly tailoring these proven methods to suit your unique lifestyle, individual needs, and specific circumstances. Whether you're navigating the demanding landscape of corporate life, striving to achieve a harmonious work-from-home existence, or simply seeking to create a more organized and peaceful environment for yourself and your family, this book will empower you with the knowledge, the tools, and the strategies you need to master the art of decluttering with grace, efficiency, and lasting success.

Welcome, then, to a journey of profound transformation, a journey that will lead you to a clutter-free existence, where every corner of your space breathes inspiration, where every object has its purpose, and where every day feels like a fresh start, brimming with possibility and potential. Let's begin this empowering endeavor together, taking it one step at a time, one small action at a time, moving forward with intention and purpose, toward a future characterized by organized serenity, unburdened potential, and the freedom to live a life that is both more productive and more deeply fulfilling.

The journey may present its challenges, but the rewards that await you—greater peace of mind, enhanced focus and concentration, increased productivity, reduced stress levels, and a harmonious balance between the demands of home and the aspirations of work–are immeasurable and will undoubtedly enrich every aspect of your life.

CHAPTER 1

IDENTIFYING YOUR CLUTTER HOTSPOTS

Maintaining a harmonious living and working environment begins with the crucial first step of identifying your clutter hotspots. Clutter, far from being merely a collection of misplaced items or a superficial mess, is a silent and insidious stressor that can gradually drain your energy, diminish your focus, and significantly reduce your overall productivity and sense of well-being. It's important to recognize that clutter often accumulates insidiously, creeping into every corner of our homes and workplaces, often without us consciously noticing its gradual encroachment. Whether it manifests as a stack of papers that never quite gets sorted, a pile of clothes perpetually waiting to be put away, or a digital inbox overflowing with a seemingly endless stream of unread messages, clutter subtly and persistently erodes our sense of control, disrupts our sense of order, and contributes to a feeling of being overwhelmed.

Clutter is not just about the physical objects that surround us; it's also about the mental and emotional baggage that accompanies them. It's about the unfinished tasks, the broken items waiting for repair, the forgotten projects, and the unfulfilled intentions that linger in our environment, creating a constant sense of unease and distraction. Recognizing the pervasive nature of clutter and understanding its multifaceted impact on our lives is the first and most essential step towards reclaiming your space, restoring a sense of clarity, and fostering a more intentional and fulfilling lifestyle.

Understanding precisely where clutter accumulates in its various forms is the first and most essential step toward reclaiming control over your environment and fostering a renewed sense of clarity and peace. Recognizing these clutter hotspots not only plays a vital role in regaining control over your physical surroundings, but also sets a solid foundation for a more intentional, purposeful, and ultimately more fulfilling lifestyle.

By strategically tackling these problem areas, systematically addressing the root causes of clutter, and implementing effective organizational strategies, you pave the way for a life that feels lighter, more organized, more manageable, and ultimately more enjoyable.

This chapter provides a comprehensive exploration of common clutter zones, those areas where clutter builds up most frequently in both personal and professional settings. It's important to understand that clutter manifests differently in different environments, and this chapter will help you gain valuable insights into the various ways that chaos and disorganization can take hold in your life. By examining both the visible and the often-hidden forms of clutter, you'll develop a deeper understanding of the multifaceted ways in which disorder can manifest in your daily life, affecting your productivity, your well-being, and your overall sense of peace.

Besides identifying clutter hotspots, we will also delve into the process of conducting a thorough and effective clutter audit, a systematic approach to assessing the state of your environment and gaining a clear understanding of the extent of your clutter challenges. We will explore practical and actionable strategies, such as the creation and utilization of visual clutter maps, which can provide a powerful visual representation of your clutter hotspots and help you prioritize your decluttering efforts more effectively. We will discuss the importance of categorizing items, not just by their physical location, but also by their function, their value, and their emotional significance, in order to prioritize your decluttering efforts with greater clarity and purpose.

By the end of this chapter, you will possess a comprehensive set of actionable steps and practical tools, effectively enabling you to remove excess clutter from your life and establish and maintain an environment that consistently promotes efficiency, fosters relaxation, and supports your overall well-being. You will gain the knowledge and the skills necessary to create a space that is not only visually appealing and organized but also conducive to productivity, creativity, and a greater sense of peace and tranquility.

Assess Personal and Workspace Clutter Zones

Clutter, as we have established, is an equal-opportunity offender; it does not discriminate based on location or lifestyle. It has the potential to infiltrate virtually every aspect of your life, from the most personal corners of your home to the most professional areas of your workspace. Therefore, understanding the specific areas where clutter accumulates in your unique environment is absolutely crucial to regaining a sense of order and control. Whether you're focusing on your personal spaces or your professional settings, it's important to recognize that different areas attract different clutter, and understanding these distinctions and nuances can make a significant difference in the effectiveness of your decluttering efforts.

In personal spaces, clutter frequently builds up in high-traffic areas, those zones that serve as the hub of daily activities and are therefore naturally prone to becoming collection points for a variety of items. Examples of these high-traffic areas include entryways, living rooms, and kitchens.

➢ **Entryways**: These areas often become magnets for items like keys, mail, shoes, bags, coats, and other miscellaneous household objects that we drop as soon as we walk through the door.

➢ **Living Room**: These spaces can accumulate a variety of clutter, from magazines and books to remote controls, electronic devices, and children's toys.

➢ **Kitchens:** These areas are susceptible to clutter because of the constant flow of food preparation, cooking, and cleaning activities. Countertops, in particular, often become cluttered with small appliances, utensils, mail, and other miscellaneous items.

Frequent daily use of these high-traffic areas causes them to become messy and disorganized quickly, thus making regular and consistent maintenance essential for clutter control.

Other personal spaces, such as bedrooms and closets, may not always exhibit the same level of visible clutter as high-traffic areas, but they can still be significant breeding grounds for hidden disorganization and accumulated excess.

➢ **Bedrooms**: These spaces can become cluttered with clothing, books, electronics, and personal items, often tucked away in drawers, under the bed, or on nightstands.

➢ **Closets:** These spaces are notorious for accumulating clothing we rarely wear, shoes we no longer use, and a variety of other items that we hold on to but seldom need or enjoy.

➢ **Bathrooms**: These areas often become stockpiled with a collection of half-used toiletries, expired medications, and an excess of beauty products, often without us realizing the sheer volume of items we have accumulated.

Workspaces, whether they are in a corporate office setting or a dedicated home office setup, present their own unique set of challenges with clutter. A cluttered desk, for example, can quickly become filled with loose papers, stacks of files, an abundance of office supplies, and a tangled mess of cords and cables, creating a visually chaotic and mentally draining environment that hinders productivity and stifles creativity.

However, it's crucial to remember that physical spaces are not the only places where clutter exists. Digital clutter can be just as disruptive and detrimental to our focus and well-being. Overloaded email inboxes, unorganized digital files, excessive notifications from various apps and platforms, and the constant barrage of information from the internet can all contribute to a sense of mental noise and overwhelm, hindering productivity, increasing stress levels, and making it difficult to concentrate on the tasks at hand.

Conduct a Clutter Audit and Self-Reflection

A clutter audit is a systematic and thorough approach to evaluating and gaining a comprehensive understanding of the clutter that exists in your life.

It involves taking a detailed inventory of different areas, both physical and digital, assessing the items you own and the information you consume, and reflecting deeply on the reasons you have kept these things in your life.

This process of self-reflection is essential, as it allows you to become more mindful of your consumption habits, to identify the underlying causes of your clutter, and to make more intentional and conscious decisions about what truly deserves to occupy space in your life.

To begin your clutter audit, start by taking a slow and deliberate walk through each room in your home and each area of your workspace, observing your surroundings with fresh and objective eyes. Approach each space as if you were seeing it for the very first time, allowing yourself to notice the details that you may have become accustomed to overlooking. Take careful note of the areas that feel the most chaotic, the most stressful, or the most difficult to navigate. Are there specific zones or corners where clutter repeatedly builds up, regardless of your previous attempts to organize them? Are there items that have remained untouched, unused, or unseen for extended periods of time, perhaps for months or even years?

As you conduct your audit, ask yourself a series of key questions about the items you encounter:

- Do I use this item regularly?
- Does this item serve a clear and practical purpose in my life?
- Does this item bring me joy, happiness, or a sense of peace?
- Or does it simply take up valuable space, both physically and mentally, contributing nothing positive to my life?

By answering these questions honestly and thoughtfully, you can make clear, informed, and intentional decisions about what items truly deserve a place in your life and what items you can confidently and comfortably let go of.

A visual clutter map is an excellent tool that can provide invaluable help in this process of conducting a clutter audit. By sketching a basic layout of your home or office and marking clutter hotspots with color-coded indicators or symbols, you can use this simple yet effective technique.

This visual representation allows you to create a tangible reference point for prioritizing the areas that require the most immediate attention and focused decluttering efforts. This visual map can also serve as a powerful source of motivation, providing a clear and interesting roadmap toward achieving a more organized and clutter-free space.

Differentiate Between Functional and Non-Functional Items

One of the most effective and transformative strategies in the journey of decluttering is to develop the ability to clearly and consistently differentiate between items that serve a functional purpose in your life and those items that no longer serve any real or meaningful purpose, but continue to occupy valuable space. Understanding this crucial distinction is essential for effectively reducing excess possessions, streamlining your environment, and creating a living and working space that truly aligns with your needs, your goals, and your values.

❖ **Defining Functional Items.**

Functional items are those objects and possessions that actively contribute to your daily life by making your tasks easier, more efficient, or more enjoyable. These items seamlessly integrate into your daily routine, providing tangible benefits and enhancing your ability to perform everyday activities.

A coffee maker that you use every morning to brew your favorite coffee is a prime example of a functional item.

A comfortable and supportive chair that promotes good posture while you work at your desk is another example of a functional object that contributes to your well-being and productivity.

People consider a set of tools that you use regularly for home repairs or DIY projects to be functional items, as they enable you to maintain your home and accomplish necessary tasks.

Their utility, their practicality, and their ability to enhance your daily life meaningfully characterize functional items.

❖ **Recognizing Non-Functional Clutter.**

Conversely, non-functional clutter comprises those items that no longer serve any real or meaningful purpose in your life, but continue to take up valuable space, both physically and mentally. These items may have once been useful or valuable, but they have now become obsolete, broken, or simply no longer relevant to your current needs and lifestyle.

Examples of non-functional clutter include broken electronics you haven't gotten around to repairing, clothing items that no longer fit or that you haven't worn in years, unread books that you have no intention of reading, and outdated paperwork or documents that are no longer needed.

Many people hold on to non-functional items for a variety of reasons, including emotional attachment to the past, a fear of scarcity or of needing the item in the future, or the persistent but often unrealistic idea that they might use the item "one day." However, learning to let go of these non-functional items, consciously choosing to release them from your possession, can lead to a more streamlined, organized, and stress-free environment, both physically and mentally.

❖ Using a Decision Matrix.

A decision matrix can be an incredibly effective tool in the process of determining what items to keep and what items to discard during your decluttering efforts. This structured and objective approach helps to remove emotional bias from the decision-making process, making it easier to part with unnecessary possessions and to make clear and rational choices about what truly deserves a place in your life.

To create a decision matrix, you can assign scores or ratings to each item based on a set of predetermined factors that are important to you. These factors might include:

Frequency of Use: How often do you use this item?

➤ **Practicality:** Does this item serve a practical purpose in your life?

➤ **Sentimental Value:** Does this item hold significant emotional value for you?

➤ **Replacement Cost**: How much would it cost to replace this item if you needed it in the future?

Storage Space Required: How much space does this item require storing?

By assigning scores to each item based on these factors, you can create a numerical representation of its value and importance in your life. This numerical data can then make more aim and less emotionally driven decisions about what to keep and what to discard.

Identify High-affected Areas for Immediate Focus

For maximum efficiency and effectiveness in your decluttering efforts, it's essential to identify the high-affected areas in your home or workspace, those areas that will yield the most significant and noticeable results when decluttered. Focusing your initial efforts on these high-affected areas allows you to see tangible and motivating results relatively quickly, providing you with the encouragement and momentum needed to continue the decluttering process with renewed enthusiasm.

A useful concept to consider in this context is the 80/20 Rule, also known as the Pareto Principle, which suggests that approximately 20% of your clutter is likely responsible for 80% of your stress, anxiety, and feelings of overwhelm. By focusing your attention on addressing this critical 20% of clutter first, you can achieve significant progress in reducing your overall stress levels and improving the functionality and organization of your space with a relatively small amount of effort.

People frequently identify entryways, kitchens, and workspaces as high-affected zones where even small and targeted changes can make a dramatic difference in the overall feeling of order and organization.

➢ **Entryways**: Decluttering your entryway can create a more welcoming and organized first impression for both yourself and your guests.

➢ **Kitchens:** Decluttering your kitchen countertops and work surfaces can significantly improve the efficiency and enjoyment of your cooking and meal preparation experiences.

➢ **Workspaces:** Decluttering your desk and organizing your work materials can dramatically enhance your productivity, focus, and overall sense of calm while working.

By strategically decluttering these high-affected areas first, you can create a powerful ripple effect that inspires and motivates you to continue the process of organization and decluttering throughout the rest of your home and office.

Maintaining a Clutter-Free Lifestyle

Decluttering, as we have emphasized throughout this chapter, is not a onetime event or a quick fix; it's an ongoing process, a continuous journey that requires mindfulness, intention, and consistent effort to maintain a clutter-free and organized lifestyle. To successfully maintain a clutter-free environment over the long term, it's essential to establish sustainable daily and weekly habits that prevent clutter from accumulating.

Simple yet effective practices, such as consistently returning items to their designated spots immediately after use, conducting regular and scheduled purging sessions to remove unwanted or unused items, and practicing mindful consumption to avoid bringing unnecessary items into your home, can all contribute significantly to sustaining an organized and clutter-free space.

Besides these habits, adopting smart and efficient storage solutions can also play a crucial role in enhancing space efficiency and maintaining organization.

Multi-functional furniture, vertical storage options that maximize vertical space, and drawer organizers that keep smaller items neatly contained can all help to optimize your space while ensuring that your belongings are easily accessible and readily available when you need them.

FINAL THOUGHTS

This chapter has provided a comprehensive and in-depth look at the multifaceted nature of clutter, exploring how it accumulates in various areas of our lives, emphasizing the importance of identifying individual clutter hotspots, and outlining the practical steps necessary to regain control over your physical and mental space. By developing a thorough understanding of clutter, by implementing structured and proven strategies for decluttering, and by establishing sustainable habits for maintaining organization, you can create an environment that not only enhances your productivity and fosters mental clarity but also significantly improves your overall well-being and contributes to a greater sense of peace and tranquility in your life.

As you continue forward on this transformative journey of decluttering, it's important to remember that the goal is not to achieve an unrealistic or unattainable state of perfection. Rather, the focus should be on creating a space that effectively supports your best life, a space that nurtures your growth, inspires your creativity, and allows you to live with greater intention and purpose. Remember that small, consistent, and sustainable efforts will ultimately yield long-lasting and profound results, helping you to build a home and a workspace that feels peaceful, functional, inspiring, and truly reflective of your authentic self.

CHAPTER 2

SETTING REALISTIC DECLUTTERING GOALS

Embarking on a decluttering journey is an exciting endeavor, a commitment to creating a more organized, functional, and peaceful living and working environment. However, like any significant undertaking, it's essential to approach it with a simple strategy and a realistic mindset. Setting realistic decluttering goals is not merely about having a vague desire to "get organized"; it's about establishing a structured framework that guides your efforts, provides a sense of direction, and ensures that you stay motivated and focused throughout the process.

The power of setting realistic goals lies in its ability to break down a potentially overwhelming task into manageable and achievable steps. Don't let the prospect of decluttering your entire home or office at once daunt you; focus instead on smaller, more specific, and reasonably achievable targets. This approach not only makes the task feel less intimidating but also allows you to experience a sense of accomplishment and progress as you achieve each goal, fueling your motivation to continue.

Setting realistic goals helps you to define your priorities and make conscious decisions about what you truly want to achieve through decluttering. It allows you to identify your specific needs, your desired outcomes, and the areas of your life that will benefit most from a more organized and clutter-free environment. To ensure your decluttering efforts align with your values and contribute to your overall well-being, clarify your intentions and set clear objectives.

This chapter will guide you through the process of setting effective and realistic decluttering goals. To ensure your goals are well-defined, measurable, achievable, relevant, and time-bound, we will explore the importance of using proven goal-setting frameworks like SMART criteria.

We will also discuss the significance of tailoring your goals to fit your unique lifestyle, your individual needs, and your specific circumstances, recognizing that there is no one-size-fits-all approach to decluttering.

We will delve into practical strategies for maintaining motivation throughout your decluttering journey, addressing potential challenges, and developing effective habits that support a clutter-free lifestyle.

By the end of this chapter, you will have the knowledge and tools to set realistic and empowering decluttering goals that will guide you toward a more organized, functional, and fulfilling environment. You will learn how to approach decluttering with intention, purpose, and a sense of confidence, transforming it from a daunting task into a rewarding and transformative journey.

❖ The Importance of Goal Setting in Decluttering

Goal setting plays a vital role in decluttering, providing structure, motivation, and a clear sense of direction. Without defined goals, decluttering can easily become an aimless and overwhelming task, leading to frustration and a lack of progress. Setting specific objectives transforms the abstract idea of "getting organized" into a series of achievable steps, making the entire process feel more manageable and less daunting.

❖ Structure and Direction

Goals provide a framework that guides your decluttering efforts, helping you to stay focused and avoid getting sidetracked. They define what you want to achieve, whether it's decluttering a specific room, organizing a particular area, or reducing the overall amount of clutter in your home. This structure helps you prioritize tasks and allocate your time and energy effectively.

❖ Motivation and Momentum

Achieving goals, even small ones, provides a sense of accomplishment and boosts motivation. Each completed task and each decluttered space serve as a tangible reminder of your progress, encouraging you to continue. Breaking down a large decluttering project into smaller, achievable goals creates a sense of momentum, making the process feel less overwhelming and more rewarding.

❖ Clarity and Focus

Goal setting helps you clarify your intentions and define what you truly want to achieve through decluttering. It prompts you to consider your priorities, your needs, and your desired outcomes. This clarity of purpose ensures that your values align with your decluttering efforts and that these efforts contribute to your overall well-being.

❖ Measuring Progress

Goals provide a benchmark for measuring your progress. By setting specific and measurable objectives, you can track your achievements and see how far you've come. This allows you to stay accountable, adjust your approach as needed, and celebrate your successes along the way.

❖ Using Effective Goal-Setting Frameworks

To ensure that your decluttering goals are effective and contribute to your success, it's essential to use proven goal-setting frameworks. These frameworks provide a structured approach to defining your objectives, making them clear, achievable, and motivating.

❖ The SMART Criteria

The SMART criteria are a widely recognized and highly effective goal-setting framework that can apply to decluttering with brilliant success. SMART is an acronym that stands for:

➢ **Specific:** Your goals should be clear and well-defined, avoiding vague or general statements. Instead of saying "I want to declutter my house," specify which areas you want to focus on, such as "I want to declutter my bedroom closet" or "I want to organize my home office desk."

➢ **Measurable:** Your goals should be quantifiable, allowing you to track your progress and determine when you have achieved them. For example, instead of saying "I want to get rid of some clothes," specify "I want to donate two bags of clothing" or "I want to reduce the number of items in my closet by 50%."

➢ **Achievable**: Your goals should be realistic and attainable, considering your current circumstances, your available time and resources, and your skill level. Avoid setting goals that are so ambitious that they are likely to lead to frustration and discouragement.

➢ You should align your goals with your overall values, needs, and desired outcomes. They should contribute to your overall well-being and help you create the environment you want to live or work in.

➢ **Time-bound**: Your goals should have a defined timeframe, providing a sense of urgency and helping you stay on track. Set specific deadlines for completing each decluttering task, such as "I will declutter my desk this weekend" or "I will organize my pantry by the end of the month."

❖ **Other Goal-Setting Methods**

Besides the SMART criteria, other goal-setting methods can also be valuable in your decluttering journey.

➢ **Backward Planning**: This method involves starting with your desired result and then working backward to identify the steps needed to achieve it. For example, if your goal is to have a completely organized home office by the end of the year, you can break down the project into smaller tasks and set deadlines for each task, working backward from the final deadline.

> **WOOP (Wish, Outcome, Obstacle, Plan):** This method encourages you to identify your wish, visualize the positive outcome of achieving it, consider the obstacles that might prevent you from reaching your goal, and create a plan to overcome those obstacles. This method can be helpful for addressing the psychological barriers that often arise during the decluttering process.

❖ **Tailoring Goals to Different Lifestyles**

It's crucial to recognize that there is no one-size-fits-all approach to decluttering goals. You should adapt your goals to your unique lifestyle, individual needs, specific circumstances, and personal preferences.

❖ **Goals for Busy Parents**

Busy parents often have limited time and energy for decluttering. Their goals might focus on quick wins and high-affected areas, such as.

Decluttering one drawer or shelf per day

Creating a designated drop zone for kids' belongings

Involving children in the decluttering process by setting aside a few minutes each day to tidy up their toys together

❖ **Goals for Students**

Students may focus on decluttering their study spaces, organizing their digital files, and managing their time effectively. Their goals might include:

➢ Organizing their notes and textbooks

➢ Creating a clutter-free study area

➢ Decluttering their computer desktop and files

➢ Setting aside specific times for studying and decluttering

❖ **Goals for Retirees**

Retirees may have more time for decluttering but may also face challenges related to downsizing or dealing with sentimental items. Their goals might include:

➤ Decluttering one room or area at a time

➤ Sorting through and organizing memorabilia

➤ Donating or selling unwanted items

➤ Creating a more manageable and accessible living space

❖ **Goals for People with Disabilities**

Individuals with disabilities may need to adapt their decluttering goals and strategies to accommodate their specific needs and limitations. Their goals might focus on:

➤ Creating accessible storage solutions

➤ Simplifying their living space for easier navigation

➤ Seeking help from family members, friends, or professional organizers

➤ Focusing on decluttering one small area at a time

❖ **Maintaining Motivation Throughout the Decluttering Process**

Maintaining motivation is essential for successfully completing your decluttering journey. The process can be challenging, and it's important to have strategies in place to keep you inspired and on track.

❖ **Visualization and Positive Self-Talk**

Visualization: Imagine the positive outcomes of decluttering, such as a more organized and peaceful home, increased productivity, and reduced stress. Visualize yourself enjoying these benefits to stay motivated.

Positive Self-Talk: Encourage yourself with positive affirmations and remind yourself of the reasons you started decluttering. Replace negative thoughts with positive and empowering self-talk.

❖ **Reward Systems**

Set up a reward system to celebrate your achievements and milestones along the way. Reward yourself with something you enjoy after completing a decluttering task. This can help make the process more enjoyable and motivating.

❖ **Overcoming Setbacks and Avoiding Burnout**

➢ **Overcoming Setbacks**: It's normal to experience setbacks during the decluttering process. Don't get discouraged by temporary setbacks. Acknowledge them, learn from them, and get back on track.

➢ **Avoiding Burnout**: Avoid trying to do too much too soon. Pace yourself, take breaks when needed, and celebrate minor victories. Don't be afraid to adjust your goals or your schedule if you felt overwhelmed.

❖ **The Role of Habits.**

Habits play a crucial role in both clutter accumulation and clutter prevention. Understanding how habits contribute to clutter and developing new habits that support a clutter-free lifestyle is essential for long-term success.

➢ **Habit Stacking:** This technique involves attaching a new habit to an existing habit. For example, you

46

could stack the habit of putting away your shoes immediately after entering the house into your existing habit of taking off your shoes.

➢ **Developing New Routines**: Create daily or weekly routines that incorporate decluttering tasks. This could include spending 15 minutes each evening tidying up or setting aside time each week for a more thorough decluttering session.

FINAL THOUGHTS

Setting realistic decluttering goals is a fundamental step in creating a more organized and fulfilling environment. By utilizing effective goal-setting frameworks, tailoring your goals to your lifestyle, and maintaining motivation throughout the process, you can transform decluttering from an overwhelming task into a rewarding and achievable journey. Remember that progress, not perfection, is the key, and each small step you take brings you closer to creating a space that supports your well-being and enhances your life.

CHAPTER 3

QUICK WINS FOR IMMEDIATE IMPACT

In the journey of decluttering, it's often the initial steps that feel the most daunting. The sheer scale of the task ahead can be overwhelming, and it's easy to get bogged down in the details before you even see tangible results. This is where the power of quick wins comes into play. Small, easily achievable decluttering tasks, completed in a short time, are quick wins. These provide a sense of accomplishment, boost motivation, and create an immediate positive impact on your environment.

The beauty of quick wins lies in their ability to generate momentum. By focusing on small, manageable tasks, you can break the cycle of procrastination and see tangible progress almost immediately. Each completed task, no matter how small, provides a sense of accomplishment and fuels your desire to continue. This positive reinforcement is crucial, especially in the early stages of decluttering, when it's easy to feel discouraged by the sheer volume of clutter that needs to be addressed.

Quick wins can have a significant impact on your overall sense of well-being. Even a small amount of decluttering can create a more organized and visually appealing environment, which can reduce stress levels, improve focus, and enhance your overall mood. By focusing on high-affected areas, you can maximize the benefits of your efforts, creating a positive ripple effect that extends beyond the immediate task at hand.

This chapter will provide you with a variety of quick win decluttering strategies you can easily incorporate into your daily routine. We will explore the concept of the "One-Minute Rule," a highly effective technique for tackling minor tasks before they accumulate into larger problems. Next, we will examine how quick wins contribute to motivation and momentum, exploring their psychology. We will discuss strategies for emergency decluttering, so you can quickly tidy up your space when unexpected guests arrive or when you need to create a more presentable environment in a short amount of time.

By the end of this chapter, you will have a range of practical and actionable quick win decluttering techniques to create immediate positive changes in your home or workspace. You will learn how to harness the power of small actions to generate significant momentum, reduce stress, and create a more organized and inviting environment.

❖ The Power of Small Actions

In decluttering, small actions are incredibly powerful. It's often the accumulation of seemingly insignificant tasks that leads to the overwhelming feeling of being buried under clutter. Conversely, it's the consistent application of small, manageable decluttering actions that ultimately leads to lasting change and a more organized environment.

❖ Overcoming Procrastination

One of the biggest obstacles to decluttering is procrastination. The task often feels so large and daunting that it's easy to put it off indefinitely. Quick wins provide a way to break this cycle of procrastination by making the initial steps feel less intimidating. When you focus on small, achievable tasks, you're more likely to take action, and each completed task provides a sense of momentum that makes it easier to keep going.

❖ Building Momentum

Momentum is a crucial element in any successful decluttering journey. Quick wins help to build this momentum by creating a positive feedback loop. As you complete minor tasks and see tangible results, you feel a sense of accomplishment, which motivates you to take on more tasks. This positive reinforcement makes the process feel more rewarding and less burdensome.

❖ Creating a Positive Impact

Even small decluttering actions can have a significant impact on your environment and your well-being.

Clearing off a cluttered countertop, organizing a messy drawer, or tidying up a small corner of your desk can create a sense of order and calm, reducing stress and improving your overall mood. By focusing on high-affected areas, you can maximize the benefits of your efforts, seeing noticeable improvements even with minimal effort.

❖ The "One-Minute Rule,"

The "One-Minute Rule" is a highly effective technique for tackling small decluttering tasks before they accumulate into larger, more overwhelming problems. This simple rule advises that you should complete any task by taking a minute or less immediately.

❖ How the-Minute Rule Works

The-Minute Rule is based on the principle that many minor tasks, when left undone, can quickly add up to create a significant amount of clutter. By addressing these tasks immediately, you prevent them from becoming bigger problems, saving you time and effort in the long run.

❖ Examples of One-Minute Tasks

You can complete countless decluttering tasks in one minute or less. Here are some examples:

➤ Putting away a dirty dish
➤ Hanging up a coat

- ➢ Returning a book to its shelf
- ➢ Throwing away junk mail
- ➢ Wiping down a countertop
- ➢ Making your bed
- ➢ Putting dirty clothes in the laundry basket
- ➢ Filing a piece of paper
- ➢ Deleting an unnecessary email

❖ **Benefits of the-Minute Rule**

The-Minute Rule offers several benefits:

- ➢ **Prevents clutter accumulation**: By addressing minor tasks immediately, you prevent them from becoming larger problems.
- ➢ **Saves time and effort**: It's much easier to complete a minor task than to deal with a larger, more complex problem later.
- ➢ **Reduces stress**: Completing minor tasks provides a sense of accomplishment and reduces the feeling of being overwhelmed by clutter.
- ➢ **Creates a sense of order**: Even small actions contribute to a more organized and tidier environment.

❖ **The Psychology of Quick Wins**

Quick wins are not just about completing minor tasks; they also have a significant psychological impact, contributing to motivation, momentum, and a positive mindset.

❖ Increased Confidence

Each completed quick win, no matter how small, provides a sense of accomplishment and boosts confidence. This feeling of success makes you more likely to take on more challenging decluttering tasks.

❖ Enhanced Motivation

Seeing tangible results, even from small actions, is highly motivating. Quick wins provide a constant reminder that your efforts are making a difference, fueling your desire to continue decluttering.

❖ Reduced Overwhelm

Breaking down a large decluttering project into smaller, quick win tasks makes the process feel less overwhelming. Focusing on one small task at a time allows you to make progress without feeling burdened by the overall scope of the project.

❖ Positive Reinforcement

Quick wins create a positive feedback loop. Completing a task and seeing the positive result reinforces the behavior, making you more likely to repeat it. This positive reinforcement is crucial for developing consistent decluttering habits.

❖ Emergency Decluttering

Sometimes, you need to declutter quickly, whether it's because unexpected guests are arriving or you need to create a more presentable environment in a short amount of time. Emergency decluttering strategies can help you achieve a significant improvement in a short period.

❖ Focus on High-affect Areas

In an emergency decluttering situation, focus on the areas that will have the most immediate visual impact. These are often the same high-affected areas identified in Chapter 1:

➢ **Entryway:** Clear off any clutter from the entryway, such as shoes, bags, and mail.

➢ **Living Room:** Tidy up the living room by straightening cushions, putting away toys, and clearing off coffee tables.

➢ **Kitchen:** Focus on clearing countertops, washing dishes, and wiping down surfaces.

➢ **Bathroom:** Tidy up the bathroom by putting away toiletries, hanging up towels, and wiping down the sink and toilet.

❖ **The "Stuff-It" Method (Use with Caution)**

The "Stuff-It" method involves quickly gathering clutter and temporarily placing it out of sight. This method can be useful for creating a quick visual improvement, but it's important to remember that it's a temporary solution. You'll need to go back and properly declutter the "stuffed" items later. Use this method sparingly and intending to address the clutter properly at a later time.

❖ Enlist Help.

If possible, enlist the help of family members or roommates to speed up the process. Divide tasks and work together to tackle the clutter quickly.

❖ Prioritize and Delegate.

Prioritize the most visible and impactful areas. Delegate tasks to others if possible. Focus on what needs to be done immediately and leave less urgent tasks for later.

FINAL THOUGHTS

Quick wins are a powerful tool in the decluttering process. By focusing on small, achievable tasks, you can generate momentum, boost motivation, and create immediate positive changes in your environment. The "One-Minute Rule" is a highly effective technique for preventing clutter accumulation, while emergency decluttering strategies can help you quickly improve the appearance of your space when needed. Remember that even small actions can have a significant impact, and each quick win brings you closer to creating a more organized, peaceful, and fulfilling environment.

CHAPTER 4

TIME-EFFICIENT DECLUTTERING TECHNIQUES

In the fast-paced world of busy professionals, time is a precious commodity. The idea of dedicating large chunks of time to decluttering can feel overwhelming and unrealistic. However, decluttering doesn't have to be an all-consuming activity. By implementing time-efficient techniques, you can make significant progress in small increments, integrating decluttering seamlessly into your daily routine without sacrificing valuable time.

This chapter focuses on strategies for maximizing your decluttering efforts within limited time constraints. We will explore various adaptable time management techniques for decluttering, such as the Pomodoro Technique, time blocking, and the Eisenhower Matrix. These methods help you allocate your time effectively, prioritize tasks, and stay focused during your decluttering sessions.

We will discuss how to incorporate decluttering into daily transitions, those often-overlooked moments throughout the day when you can squeeze in a few minutes of tidying up. By utilizing these transition times, you can make consistent progress without having to set aside large blocks of dedicated decluttering time.

This chapter emphasizes the importance of rest and breaks during decluttering. While it's important to be efficient, it's also crucial to avoid burnout and maintain focus. We will discuss strategies for incorporating brief breaks into your decluttering sessions to ensure that you stay energized and productive.

By the end of this chapter, you will have a range of time-efficient decluttering techniques you can easily integrate into your busy schedule. You will learn how to make the most of small pockets of time, prioritize your decluttering tasks, and maintain focus and energy throughout the process.

Time Management Strategies for Decluttering

Effective time management is essential for successful decluttering, especially when you have limited time available. Adapting several time management techniques can help you allocate your time effectively, prioritize tasks, and stay focused during decluttering.

❖ **The Pomodoro Technique.**

The Pomodoro Technique is a time management method that uses focused work intervals interspersed with brief breaks. This technique can be highly effective for decluttering, helping you to maintain focus and avoid burnout.

How it Works: Set a timer for 25 minutes. Focus on decluttering during this time, without distractions. When the timer goes off, take a 5-minute break. Repeat this cycle four times. After four cycles, take a longer break off 20-30 minutes.

Benefits for Decluttering: Breaks down, decluttering into manageable chunks. Maintains focus and concentration. Prevents burnout. Provides a sense of accomplishment after each interval.

❖ Time Blocking.

Time blocking involves scheduling specific blocks of time for specific tasks. This technique can allocate dedicated time for decluttering in your daily or weekly schedule.

How it Works: Identify specific times in your schedule when you can dedicate to decluttering. Block off these times in your calendar, just like you would schedule any other important appointment. During these time blocks, focus solely on decluttering, avoiding distractions.

Benefits for decluttering: Ensures that you dedicate time to decluttering. Helps you prioritize decluttering, among other tasks. Provides a sense of structure and accountability.

❖ The Eisenhower Matrix.

The Eisenhower Matrix, also known as the Urgent-Important Matrix, is a tool for prioritizing tasks based on their urgency and importance. You can adapt this matrix to declutter, focusing first on the most impactful areas.

➤ **How it Works:** Divide your decluttering tasks into four categories: Urgent: These tasks need to be done immediately. You should schedule these important tasks for later. You may delegate or eliminate tasks that seem urgent but are not essential. We can eliminate these tasks. Focus on the "Important" and "Important but Not Urgent" tasks first.

➤ **Benefits for Decluttering:** Helps you prioritize decluttering tasks. Ensures that you focus on the most impactful areas. Prevents you from getting bogged down in less important tasks.

❖ **Decluttering During Transitions**

Daily transitions, those brief periods between activities, often present overlooked opportunities for decluttering. By utilizing these transition times, you can make consistent progress without having to set aside large blocks of dedicated time.

❖ Examples of Transition Times

Here are some examples of daily transitions that you can use for decluttering.

Waiting for appointments: While waiting for a doctor's appointment, a hair appointment, or any other scheduled appointment, you can use that time to declutter your bag, organize your wallet, or delete unnecessary emails on your phone.

During commercial breaks: While watching television, use commercial breaks to tidy up the living room, put away laundry, or clear off a countertop.

While commuting: If you commute by public transportation, you can use that time to declutter your inbox, organize your digital files, or plan your decluttering tasks for the day.

Before bed: Spend 5-10 minutes before bed tidying up your bedroom, putting away clothes, or organizing your nightstand.

First thing in the morning: Start your day with a quick decluttering session, such as making your bed, clearing off your desk, or organizing your bathroom counter.

❖ Maximizing Transition Time

To make the most of transition times, it's important to be prepared and have a plan.

Keep decluttering supplies handy: Keep small decluttering supplies, such as trash bags, donation boxes, or cleaning clothes, in convenient locations so you can easily grab them during transition times.

Have a specific task in mind: Before a transition time begins, have a specific decluttering task in mind so you can make the most of the time.

Focus on small, manageable tasks: Use transition times for small, quick tasks completable within minutes.

Be consistent: The key to success is consistency. Even small amounts of decluttering, when done consistently, can add up to significant progress.

❖ **The Importance of Rest and Breaks**

While it's important to be efficient with your decluttering time, it's also crucial to prioritize rest and breaks. Decluttering can be physically and mentally demanding, and it's essential to avoid burnout and maintain focus.

❖ **Preventing Burnout**

Trying to declutter for extended periods without breaks can lead to burnout, making the process feel overwhelming and discouraging. Taking regular breaks allows you to rest, recharge, and maintain your energy levels.

❖ **Maintaining Focus**

Short breaks can actually improve your focus and concentration. When you take a break, your mind rests and resets, allowing you to return to the task with renewed energy and clarity.

❖ **Strategies for Rest and Breaks**

Here are some strategies for incorporating rest and breaks into your decluttering sessions:

➢ **Follow the Pomodoro Technique:** As discussed earlier, the Pomodoro Technique incorporates regular brief breaks, helping you to maintain focus and avoid burnout.

➢ **Schedule breaks:** If you're not using the Pomodoro Technique, schedule brief breaks every 20-30 minutes.

➢ **Take a break when you feel overwhelmed:** If you felt overwhelmed or frustrated, it's a sign that you need to take a break. Step away from the task, do something relaxing, and return to it later with a fresh perspective.

➢ **Listen to your body**: Pay attention to your body's signals. If you're feeling tired, take a break. If you're feeling stiff, stretch or move around.

FINAL THOUGHTS

Time-efficient decluttering techniques are essential for busy professionals who want to create a more organized environment without sacrificing valuable time. By implementing time management strategies, using daily transitions, and prioritizing rest and breaks, you can make consistent progress, maintain focus, and avoid burnout. Remember that even small amounts of decluttering, when done consistently and efficiently, can lead to significant and lasting results.

CHAPTER 5

EMOTIONAL BENEFITS OF A CLUTTER-FREE SPACE

While the practical benefits of decluttering, such as increased productivity and improved organization, are clear, the emotional benefits are often just as profound, if not more so. Clutter has a significant impact on our mental and emotional well-being, and creating a clutter-free space can lead to a greater sense of calm, clarity, and overall happiness.

This chapter delves into the emotional impact of clutter and explores the positive psychological changes that occur when we declutter our physical environment. We will examine the neuroscience of clutter, exploring how it affects the brain and contributes to stress, anxiety, and other negative emotions. Understanding the neurological basis of these effects can provide a deeper appreciation for the importance of creating a clutter-free space.

We will discuss the connection between clutter and relationships, exploring how clutter can affect our interactions with family members, partners, and friends. We will also explore the powerful link between mindfulness and decluttering, discussing how mindfulness practices can enhance the decluttering process and promote long-term emotional well-being.

By the end of this chapter, you will gain a deeper understanding of the emotional benefits of a clutter-free space. You will learn how decluttering can improve your mental and emotional health, enhance your relationships, and cultivate a greater sense of peace and joy in your life.

❖ The Impact of Clutter on Mental and Emotional Well-being

Clutter is more than just a visual annoyance; it has a significant impact on our mental and emotional well-being. It can contribute to a range of negative emotions, including stress, anxiety, overwhelm, and even depression.

❖ Stress and Anxiety

Clutter creates a sense of chaos and disorganization, which can trigger the stress response in our bodies. Surrounding ourselves with clutter forces our brains to process visual stimuli constantly, leading to mental fatigue and a feeling of being overwhelmed. This can manifest as anxiety, irritability, and difficulty concentrating.

❖ Overwhelm

Clutter can make us feel overwhelmed by the sheer volume of possessions and tasks that need to be addressed. This feeling of being overwhelmed can lead to procrastination, avoidance, and a sense of being stuck.

❖ Depression

Sometimes chronic clutter can contribute to feelings of sadness, hopelessness, and depression. Clutter can create a sense of stagnation and prevent us from moving forward in our lives.

❖ The Neuroscience of Clutter

Research has shown that clutter has a measurable impact on the brain. Studies have found that clutter can overload the visual cortex, the part of the brain responsible for processing visual information. This overload can lead to decreased attention, impaired decision-making, and increased stress.

❖ Cognitive Overload

Clutter creates a visually complex environment that requires the brain to process a large amount of information. This can lead to cognitive overload, making it difficult to focus, concentrate, and think clearly.

❖ Reduced Attention Span

Clutter can distract us and reduce our attention span. Surrounding clutter constantly distracts us, hindering our ability to concentrate on the task.

❖ Impaired Decision-Making

Clutter can impair our decision-making abilities. Clutter overwhelms us, making it difficult to prioritize tasks, make choices, and solve problems effectively.

❖ Clutter and Relationships

Clutter can also have a negative impact on our relationships with family members, partners, and friends. It can create tension, conflict, and a sense of disharmony in the home.

❖ Conflict and Tension

Clutter can be a source of conflict and tension between family members or partners. Different people have different tolerances for clutter, and disagreements about cleanliness and organization can lead to arguments and resentment.

❖ Communication Difficulties

Clutter can make it difficult to communicate effectively. Clutter hinders effective communication by making it difficult to focus on conversations, which leads to misunderstandings and miscommunication.

❖ Impact on Social Life

Clutter can make us feel embarrassed about our homes, leading us to avoid inviting guests over. This can lead to social isolation and a diminished sense of connection.

❖ Mindfulness and Decluttering

Mindfulness, the practice of paying attention to the present moment without judgment, can be a powerful tool for enhancing the decluttering process and promoting long-term emotional well-being

Mindful Decluttering

Mindful decluttering involves approaching the task with intention, awareness, and non-judgment. It's about being present with the process, paying attention to your thoughts and feelings, and making conscious decisions about what to keep and what to let go.

❖ Benefits of Mindful Decluttering

Increased self-awareness: Mindful decluttering can help you become more aware of your emotional attachments to possessions and your patterns of consumption.

Reduced emotional distress: By being present with your emotions during the decluttering process, you can process them healthily and reduce the emotional distress associated with letting go.

Enhanced focus and concentration: Mindfulness practices can improve your focus and concentration, making the decluttering process more efficient and effective.

Greater sense of peace and calm: Mindful decluttering can help you create a more peaceful and calming environment, both physically and mentally.

❖ Mindfulness Practices for Decluttering

➢ **Start with awareness**: Before you declutter, take a few moments to realize your surroundings, your thoughts, and your feelings.

➢ **Focus on the present moment**: As you declutter, try to stay present with the task at hand, avoiding distractions and focusing on each item as you handle it.

➤ **Observe your thoughts and feelings**: Pay attention to the thoughts and feelings that arise as you declutter. Notice any emotional attachments you have to possessions and try to understand the reasons behind them.

➤ **Practice non-judgment:** Avoid judging yourself or your possessions. Approach the task with kindness and compassion.

➤ **Let go with gratitude:** When you decide to let go of an item, do so with gratitude for the purpose it served in your life.

FINAL THOUGHTS

The emotional benefits of a clutter-free space are significant and far-reaching. Decluttering can reduce stress, anxiety, and overwhelm, improve focus and concentration, enhance relationships, and cultivate a greater sense of peace and joy. By understanding the neuroscience of clutter and practicing mindful decluttering, you can unlock the transformative power of a clutter-free environment and create a life that is both more organized and more emotionally fulfilling.

CHAPTER 6

MINDSET SHIFTS FOR LASTING CHANGE

Decluttering is not just about physically removing items from your space; it's also about transforming your mindset and developing new ways of thinking about your possessions. Lasting change in your decluttering habits requires a shift in perspective, a willingness to challenge old beliefs, and the adoption of new, more empowering ways of thinking.

This chapter explores the mindset shifts that are essential for achieving lasting change in your decluttering journey. We will delve into techniques inspired by Cognitive-Behavioral Therapy (CBT), a powerful approach for challenging negative thoughts and beliefs that contribute to clutter accumulation. CBT techniques can help you identify and change the thought patterns that lead to hoarding, overconsumption, and difficulty letting go.

We will discuss the concept of values-based decluttering, emphasizing the importance of aligning your possessions with your core values and priorities. By clarifying what truly matters to you, you can make more intentional decisions about what to keep and what to discard, creating a space that reflects your authentic self.

This chapter will highlight the importance of self-compassion throughout the decluttering process. Decluttering can be emotionally challenging, and it's essential to approach it with kindness, understanding, and acceptance. We will explore strategies for practicing self-compassion, particularly when facing setbacks or challenges.

By the end of this chapter, you will gain a deeper understanding of the mindset shifts that are necessary for achieving lasting change in your decluttering habits. You will learn how to challenge negative thoughts, align your possessions with your values, and practice self-compassion, empowering you to create a clutter-free life that is both sustainable and fulfilling.

❖ **The Importance of Mindset in Decluttering**

Your mindset plays a crucial role in your decluttering journey. It influences your motivation, your ability to let go of possessions, and your long-term success in maintaining a clutter-free environment.

❖ Mindset as a Foundation

A positive and empowering mindset provides a firm foundation for your decluttering efforts. It helps you approach the task with confidence, resilience, and a sense of purpose.

❖ Overcoming Obstacles

A negative or limiting mindset can create obstacles to decluttering. It can lead to procrastination, emotional attachment to possessions, and difficulty deciding about what to keep and what to discard.

❖ Long-Term Success

Mindset shifts are essential for achieving long-term success in decluttering. Without a change in perspective, you may fell back into old habits and accumulating clutter again.

❖ Cognitive-Behavioral Therapy (CBT) Techniques

Cognitive-Behavioral Therapy (CBT) is a therapeutic approach that focuses on identifying and changing negative thought patterns and behaviors. CBT techniques can be highly effective in challenging the thoughts and beliefs that contribute to clutter accumulation.

❖ Identifying Negative Thoughts

The first step in CBT is to identify the negative thoughts and beliefs that you have about your possessions. These thoughts might include:

➢ "I might need this someday."

➢ "It was a gift, so I can't get rid of it."

➢ "I spent money on it, so I have to keep it."

➢ "Letting go of this means letting go of the memory."

❖ Challenging Negative Thoughts

Once you have identified your negative thoughts, you can challenge them. Ask yourself:

➢ Is this thought realistic?

➤ Is there evidence to support this thought?

➤ What is the worst that could happen if I let go of this item?

➤ What are the benefits of letting go of this item?

❖ **Replacing Negative Thoughts**

After challenging your negative thoughts, you can replace them with more positive and empowering thoughts, such as

➤ "I can always replace this if I need it."

➤ "The memory is more important than the object."

➤ "Letting go of this will free up space for things I truly love."

➤ "I am in control of my possessions, not the other way around."

❖ **Behavioral Experiments**

CBT also uses behavioral experiments to test the validity of negative thoughts. For example, if you have a fear of letting go of clothes because you might need them someday, you could conduct a behavioral experiment by donating a few items and observing whether you actually need them in the future.

❖ Values-Based Decluttering

Value-based decluttering involves aligning your possessions with your core values and priorities. This approach helps you make more intentional decisions about what to keep and what to discard, creating a space that reflects your authentic self.

❖ Identifying Your Core Values.

The first step in values-based decluttering is to identify your core values. These are the principles and beliefs that are most important to you in your life. Some common core values include:

➢ Family
➢ Health
➢ Creativity
➢ Simplicity
➢ Freedom
➢ Connection
➢ Growth

❖ Aligning Possessions with Values.

Once you have identified your core values, you can evaluate your possessions in relation to those values. Ask yourself:

Do my core values align with this item?

This contributes to the life I want, right?

Does it align with my values and bring me joy? Is it joyful and purposeful, in line with my values?

❖ **Making Intentional Decisions.**

Value-based decluttering helps you make more intentional decisions about what to keep and what to discard. If an item doesn't align with your values, it's easier to let go of it, even if it has sentimental value or is expensive.

❖ **Self-Compassion.**

Decluttering can be an emotionally challenging process. It's important to approach it with self-compassion, treating yourself with kindness, understanding, and acceptance.

❖ **Acknowledging Difficult Emotions.**

It's normal to experience a range of emotions during decluttering, such as sadness, guilt, anxiety, or fear. Acknowledge these emotions without judgment and allow yourself to feel them.

❖ **Practicing Self-Kindness.**

Treat yourself with the same kindness and understanding that you would offer to a friend who is going through a difficult time. 1 Avoid self-criticism and self-blame.

❖ **Accepting Imperfection.**

Decluttering is a process, not a destination. It's okay to make mistakes, experience setbacks, and not achieve perfection. Accept that progress takes time and be patient with yourself.

❖ **Strategies for Self-Compassion self**-soothing touch: When you're feeling overwhelmed, try placing your hand on your heart or giving yourself a gentle hug.

Mindful self-compassion: Practice mindfulness techniques to become more aware of your emotions and respond to them with kindness and understanding.

Supportive self-talk: Use positive and encouraging self-talk to combat negative thoughts and self-criticism.

FINAL THOUGHTS

Mindset shifts are essential for achieving lasting change in your decluttering habits. By challenging negative thoughts with CBT techniques, aligning your possessions with your values, and practicing self-compassion, you can transform your relationship with your belongings and create a clutter-free life that is both sustainable and fulfilling. Remember that decluttering is a journey of self-discovery and personal growth, and a positive and compassionate mindset is your most valuable tool.

CHAPTER 7

CREATING A SUSTAINABLE DECLUTTERING SYSTEM

Decluttering is not a onetime event; it's an ongoing process; a lifestyle shift that requires the establishment of sustainable systems and habits. Staying organized requires consistent effort and strategies that fit your goals.

This chapter delves into the intricacies of creating a sustainable decluttering system, providing a comprehensive guide to establishing routines, implementing effective storage solutions, and adapting your organizational strategies to different life stages. We will explore the importance of developing daily, weekly, and monthly maintenance routines that prevent clutter from accumulating and ensure that your space remains organized and functional.

We will provide an in-depth exploration of various storage solutions, examining different containers, shelving options, and furniture with built-in storage. We will discuss the principles of effective storage, including the importance of labeling, accessibility, and maximizing space utilization. Addressing the challenges of decluttering and organizing small spaces, we will offer specific strategies for maximizing limited square footage.

This chapter will explore the importance of adapting your decluttering system to different life stages. As your needs, priorities, and living circumstances change, your organizational strategies must develop to remain effective. We will discuss how to adjust your systems for various life transitions, such as moving, getting married, having children, or downsizing.

By the end of this chapter, you will have a comprehensive set of strategies and tools for creating a sustainable decluttering system. You will learn how to establish effective routines, implement practical storage solutions, adapt your systems to different life stages, and cultivate long-term habits that support a clutter-free lifestyle.

❖ **Establishing Effective Maintenance Routines.**

Creating a sustainable decluttering system hinge on the establishment of consistent maintenance routines. These routines, incorporated into your daily, weekly, and monthly schedules, act as preventative measures, preventing clutter from accumulating and ensuring that your space remains organized and functional.

❖ **Daily Maintenance Routines.**

Daily maintenance routines are the foundation of a clutter-free lifestyle. These small, consistent actions, performed regularly, prevent clutter from building up and keep your space feeling fresh and tidy.

➢ **The 5-Minute Tidy**: Dedicate 5 minutes each day to a quick tidy-up. Focus on high-traffic areas, putting items back in their place, clearing off surfaces, and addressing any immediate clutter hotspots. You could do this before leaving for work, after dinner, or before bed.

➢ **The-Touch Rule**: Apply the "One-Touch Rule" to incoming items. This rule states you should handle an item only once. For example, when you receive mail, sort it immediately, discard junk mail, and file important documents. When you take off your shoes, put them away. This prevents items from being set down and left to accumulate.

➢ **Make Your Bed:** Making your bed each morning is a simple yet powerful habit that can instantly make your bedroom feel more organized and tidier. It sets a positive tone for the day and encourages a sense of order.

➢ **Clear Surfaces:** Regularly clear off surfaces, such as countertops, tables, and desks. Avoid letting items pile up. Put things away immediately after use.

➢ **Dish Duty:** Don't let dishes accumulate in the sink. Wash dishes after each meal or load them into the dishwasher. A clean sink makes a big difference in the overall feeling of order in the kitchen.

❖ Weekly Maintenance Routines.

Weekly maintenance routines allow for a more thorough tidy-up and enable addressing areas overlooked during the daily routine.

➤ **The Weekly Reset**: Designate a specific time each week for a more in-depth decluttering session. This could be an hour on a Saturday morning or a few shorter sessions spread throughout the week. Focus on one room or area at a time, tackling tasks such as dusting and vacuuming cleaning bathrooms, organizing drawers and shelves dealing with accumulated paperwork putting away laundry.

➤ **Meal Planning and Grocery Organization:** Plan your meals for the week and organize your pantry and refrigerator accordingly. This helps to prevent food waste and makes meal preparation more efficient.

➤ **Digital Declutter**: Dedicate some time each week to digital decluttering. This could include: Organizing computer files Deleting unnecessary emails Unsubscribing from unwanted newsletters Backing up important data.

❖ Monthly Maintenance Routines.

Monthly maintenance routines allow you to address less frequent tasks and perform a more comprehensive review of your organizational systems.

➤ **Monthly Decluttering Focus:** Choose a specific area of your home or office to focus on each month. This could be a closet, a storage room, or a specific category of items, such as books or electronics. This allows you to tackle larger decluttering projects in manageable chunks.

➤ **Storage Review:** Review your storage systems and make sure they are still working effectively. Reorganize or adjust as needed. Discard any items that are no longer needed or used.

➤ **Deep Cleaning:** Perform a more thorough cleaning of your home, including tasks such as Washing windows Cleaning appliances Shampooing carpets Washing curtains or blinds.

➤ **Financial Review**: Review your finances and declutter any unnecessary subscriptions or expenses.

❖ Implementing Effective Storage Solutions

Effective storage solutions are crucial for maintaining organization and preventing clutter from re-accumulating. The right storage solutions can maximize space utilization, keep items easily accessible, and create a sense of order and calm.

❖ Types of Storage Containers

Choosing the right storage containers is essential for organizing your belongings effectively. Consider the following options:

➤ **Bins and Baskets**: Versatile and practical bins and baskets can store a wide variety of items. Choose bins and baskets that are appropriately sized for the items you want to store and that fit well in your storage spaces.

➤ **Drawers and Organizers:** Drawers and organizers are ideal for keeping smaller items contained and preventing them from getting lost or cluttered. Drawer dividers, drawer inserts, and small containers can help to maximize drawer space and keep items neatly arranged.

➢ **Shelving Units:** Shelving units provide valuable vertical storage space and can store a wide range of items, from books and decorative objects to clothing and supplies. Choose to shelve units that are appropriate for the space and the items you want to store.

➢ **Boxes and Containers with Lids:** Boxes and containers with lids are useful for storing items you don't need to access frequently or for protecting items from dust and damage. Empty containers are helpful for easily seeing what's inside.

❖ **Shelving Options**

Shelving is a fundamental element of effective storage. Consider these options:

➢ **Bookshelves:** Traditional and versatile, bookshelves can store books, decorative items, and a variety of other belongings.

➢ **Wall Shelves:** Wall shelves are a great way to use vertical space and create a visually appealing display. They can store books, plants, photos, and other decorative items.

- ➤ **Adjustable Shelving Units:** You can customize adjustable shelving units to fit your specific needs. You can adjust the shelves to different heights to accommodate items of various sizes.
- ➤ **Floating Shelves:** Floating shelves create a clean and modern look and can display decorative items or store small objects.

❖ **Furniture with Built-In Storage**

Choosing furniture with built-in storage is a smart way to maximize space and keep clutter at bay.

- ➤ **Storage Beds:** Beds with built-in drawers or compartments under the mattress provide valuable storage space for bedding, clothing, or other items.
- ➤ **Ottomans with storage:** Ottomans with lift-up lids or drawers offer a convenient way to store blankets, pillows, or other items in your living room.
- ➤ **Benches with Storage:** Benches with built-in storage are useful for entryways, mudrooms, or bedrooms, providing a place to sit and store items such as shoes, bags, or toys.
- ➤ **7.2.4 Vertical Storage Solutions.**

➤ Using vertical space is essential for maximizing storage, especially in small spaces.

➤ **Wall-Mounted Organizers**: Wall-mounted organizers can store a variety of items, such as tools, office supplies, or kitchen utensils.

➤ **Over-the-Door Organizers**: Over-the-door organizers are a simple and effective way to use the space on the back of doors. They can store shoes, accessories, or cleaning supplies.

➤ **Tall Shelving Units:** Tall shelving units reach closer to the ceiling, providing more storage space than shorter units.

❖ **Principles of Effective Storage**

Besides choosing the right storage solutions, it's important to follow some key principles of effective storage:

➤ **Maximize Space Utilization:** Use every available space, including corners, walls, and under furniture.

➤ **Accessibility:** Arrange your storage so that frequently used items are easily accessible.

➤ Visibility: Make sure you can easily see what you have stored. Empty containers and proper labeling can help with this.

➤ **Labeling:** Label storage containers clearly and consistently. This will help you find items quickly and easily.

➤ **Categorization:** Group similar items together. This makes it easier to find what you need and prevents items from getting lost.

➤ **Regular Purging:** Regularly review your storage and discard any items that are no longer needed or used. This prevents clutter from re-accumulating.

❖ **Decluttering and Organizing in Small Spaces**

Decluttering and organizing in small spaces present unique challenges, but with creative solutions and strategic planning, it's possible to maximize space and create a functional and comfortable living environment.

❖ **Multifunctional Furniture**

Choosing furniture that serves multiple purposes is essential for maximizing space in small homes.

➢ **Sofa Beds:** Sofa beds offer comfortable seating during the day and convert into a bed at night.

➢ **Folding Tables:** Use folding tables when needed, then store them away when not in use.

➢ **Nesting Tables:** Use nesting tables individually or stack them to save space.

Using Vertical Space.

As mentioned earlier, using vertical space is crucial to small spaces.

➢ **Floor-to-Ceiling Shelving:** Maximize storage by using shelving units that reach from the floor to the ceiling.

➢ **Wall-Mounted Storage:** use wall space for storage with shelves, cabinets, and organizers.

❖ **Creating Zones.**

In small spaces, it's helpful to create distinct zones for different activities.

➢ **Define Areas:** Use rugs, furniture arrangement, or dividers to define different areas, such as a living area, dining area, or workspace.

➢ **Multipurpose Zones:** Consider how zones can serve multiple purposes. For example, people can also use a dining table as a workspace.

❖ **Optimizing Storage.**

Optimize storage by using every available space and implementing clever storage solutions.

➢ **Under-Bed Storage:** use the space under your bed for storage with drawers, containers, or bed risers.

➢ **Behind-the-Door Storage:** Use organizers or hooks on the back of doors for storage.

Corner Storage: use corner spaces with corner shelves or cabinets.

❖ **Minimizing Clutter.**

In small spaces, it's especially important to minimize clutter.

➢ **Be Selective:** Be selective about what you bring into your home. Only keep items that you truly need, use, or love.

➢ **Regular Purging:** Regularly declutter and get rid of items you no longer need.

➤ **Digital Declutter**: Keep your digital space organized to minimize mental clutter.

❖ **Adapting Your System to Different Life Stages**

Your decluttering and organizational needs will change throughout different life stages. It's important to adapt your systems to remain effective and meet your developing needs.

❖ **Moving.**

Moving is a natural time to declutter and reorganize.

➤ **Pre-Move Declutter:** Declutter before you move to avoid packing and transporting unnecessary items.

➤ **New Space Planning:** Plan the layout of your additional space and determine your storage needs before you unpack.

➤ **Unpack Strategically**: Unpack one room at a time, focusing on essential items first.

❖ **Getting Married or moving in with a Partner.**

Combining households often requires decluttering and merging belongings.

- ➢ **Joint Decluttering**: Declutter together, discussing what items to keep and what to discard.
- ➢ **Shared Storage:** Create shared storage spaces and systems that work for both of you.
- ➢ **Compromise:** Be willing to compromise and respect each other's belongings and organizational styles.

❖ **Having Children.**

Children bring new challenges and opportunities for decluttering and organizing.

- ➢ **Toy Rotation:** Rotate toys to keep them fresh and prevent clutter.
- ➢ **Designated Play Areas:** Create designated play areas with storage for toys and games.
- ➢ **Regular Toy Decluttering**: Regularly declutter toys, donating or discarding items that are no longer used.

❖ **Downsizing.**

Downsizing requires a significant decluttering effort.

- ➢ **Prioritize Essentials:** Prioritize essential items and let go of non-essential belongings.
- ➢ **Measure Your Space:** Measure your additional space and plan how your furniture and belongings will fit.
- ➢ **Consider Your Lifestyle**: Consider your alternative lifestyle and what items you will need or use in your new home.
- ❖ **Empty, nesting.**

When children leave home, it's a good time to declutter and reorganize.

- ➢ **Reclaim Spaces**: Reclaim spaces that were previously used by children.
- ➢ **Re-evaluate needs**: Re-evaluate your storage needs and adjust your systems accordingly.
- ➢ **Pursue Hobbies**: Create spaces for hobbies and activities you enjoy.
- ❖ **Maintaining a Clutter-Free Life Long Term**

Maintaining a clutter-free life is a continuous journey that requires ongoing effort and commitment.

- ➤ **Mindful Consumption**: Be mindful of what you bring into your home. Avoid impulsive purchases and only buy items that you truly need, use, or love.
- ➤ **Regular Decluttering**: Continue to declutter regularly, even after you have achieved your initial decluttering goals.
- ➤ **Consistent Routines**: Stick to your daily, weekly, and monthly maintenance routines.
- ➤ **Adaptability:** Be willing to adapt your systems and strategies as your needs and circumstances change.
- ➤ **Patience and persistence**: Be patient with yourself and persistent in your efforts. Maintaining a clutter-free life is a marathon, not a sprint.

FINAL THOUGHTS

Creating a sustainable decluttering system is essential for achieving lasting order and maintaining a clutter-free lifestyle. By establishing effective maintenance routines, implementing practical storage solutions, adapting your systems to different life stages, and cultivating long-term habits, you can create a home that is both organized and functional, supporting your well-being and enhancing your quality of life. Sticking with it, being flexible, and taking the initiative are important for long-term success.

CHAPTER 8

OPTIMIZING YOUR WORK-FROM-HOME SPACE

The rise of remote work has revolutionized the way we approach our professional lives, offering greater flexibility, autonomy, and the opportunity to design a work environment that suits our individual needs and preferences. However, with this newfound freedom comes the challenge of creating a dedicated and productive workspace within the confines of our homes. A well-designed work-from-home space is essential for maximizing productivity, minimizing distractions, and maintaining a healthy work-life balance.

This chapter provides a comprehensive guide to optimizing your work-from-home space, addressing key aspects such as design principles, technology integration, and creating a motivating environment. We will explore the fundamental principles of effective home office design, including the importance of lighting, ergonomics, acoustics, color psychology, and biophilia design. Understanding these principles will empower you to create a workspace that is both functional and aesthetically pleasing, promoting focus, creativity, and well-being.

This study will examine the role of technology in the home office, exploring its capacity to both boost and impede productivity. We will provide practical tips for using technology effectively, minimizing distractions, managing digital clutter, and creating a healthy relationship with digital devices. We will also address the importance of cybersecurity and data protection in the work-from-home environment.

This chapter will explore strategies for creating a motivating and inspiring home office environment. We will discuss the importance of personalization, incorporating elements that reflect your personal style and interests, and creating a space that fosters creativity, focus, and a sense of purpose. We will also address the challenges of maintaining motivation and productivity in the home office, providing tips for overcoming distractions, setting boundaries, and avoiding burnout.

By the end of this chapter, you will have a comprehensive set of strategies and tools for optimizing your work-from-home space. You will learn how to design a functional and aesthetically pleasing workspace, integrate technology effectively, create a motivating environment, and cultivate habits that support productivity, well-being, and a healthy work-life balance.

❖ Home Office Design Principles

Creating an effective work-from-home space starts with understanding and applying sound design principles. These principles guide the layout, aesthetics, and functionality of your workspace, ensuring that it supports your productivity, comfort, and well-being.

❖ Lighting

Proper lighting is crucial for a productive and comfortable home office. Inadequate lighting can lead to eyestrain, headaches, and fatigue, while excessive or harsh lighting can cause glare and discomfort.

➢ **Natural Light:** Maximize natural light. Position your desk near a window to take advantage of daylight. Natural light is not only beneficial for your eyes but also improves mood and reduces energy consumption.

➢ **Artificial Light:** Supplement natural light with appropriate artificial lighting. Ambient **Lighting:** Provide general illumination for the room. This could be from an overhead light fixture or floor lamp. Task Lighting: Focuses light on your work area. A desk lamp with an adjustable arm is ideal for task lighting, allowing you to direct the light where you need it most. Accent Lighting: Used to highlight specific features or create a desired mood.

➢ **Light Temperature:** Choose light bulbs with a color temperature that is conducive to work. For work areas, recommend cool white or daylight bulbs (5000-6500K) because they promote alertness and focus.

➢ **Glare Reduction:** Minimize glare by positioning your computer screen away from direct sunlight and using window coverings such as blinds or curtains to control the amount of light entering the room.

❖ **Ergonomics.**

Ergonomics focuses on designing workspaces and equipment to fit the human body, reducing the risk of injuries and promoting comfort.

➢ **Chair:** Invest in a high-quality ergonomic chair that provides proper lumbar support, adjustable height, armrests, and a comfortable seat. Your feet should be flat on the floor or supported by a footrest.

➢ **Desk:** Choose a desk that is the height of your chair. Your elbows should be at a 90-degree angle when typing. Consider a standing desk or a desk converter to allow for standing while working.

➢ **Monitor Placement**: Position your monitor at arm's length, with the top of the screen at or slightly below eye level. This helps to prevent neck strain. Use a monitor stand or adjustable arm to achieve the correct height and position.

➢ **Keyboard and Mouse:** Position your keyboard and mouse so that your wrists are straight and your forearms are parallel to the floor. Use a keyboard tray if necessary. Consider an ergonomic keyboard and mouse to reduce strain.

➢ **Breaks and movement**: Take regular breaks to stand up, stretch, and move around. Even brief breaks can help to prevent fatigue and discomfort.

❖ **Acoustics**

Noise and distractions can significantly affect productivity in a home office. Creating a space with good acoustics can help to minimize distractions and create a more focused environment.

Identify Noise Sources: Identify potential sources of noise, both inside and outside your home.

➢ **Sound Absorption:** Use materials that absorb sound, such as Rugs: Area rugs can help to absorb sound and reduce echoes. Curtains and Blinds: Soft window coverings can help to dampen sound. Install acoustic panels on walls or ceilings to absorb sound waves. **Upholstered Furniture:** Upholstered furniture can also help to absorb sound.

➢ **Soundproofing:** If necessary, consider soundproofing measures, such as Sealing Gaps: Seal any gaps around doors and windows to prevent sound from entering or leaving the room. Adding

Mass: Adding mass to walls or ceilings can help to block sound transmission.

➢ **White Noise:** If you can't eliminate all noise, consider using a white noise machine or app to mask distracting sounds.

❖ **Color Psychology.**

Color has a powerful impact on our mood and emotions. Choosing the right colors for your home office can help to create a desired atmosphere and enhance productivity.

➢ **Cool Colors:** Cool colors, such as blue, green, and purple, are calming and conducive to focus and concentration. Light shades of these colors are effective for creating a peaceful and productive environment.

➢ **Warm Colors:** Yellow, orange, and red energize and stimulate, but can also overwhelm if used in large quantities. Use warm colors as accents to add pops of energy and creativity.

➢ **Neutral Colors:** Neutral colors, such as white, gray, and beige, provide a clean and versatile backdrop.

They can create a sense of spaciousness and allow other colors to stand out.

➤ **Preference:** Ultimately, the best colors for your home office are those that you find appealing and that create the atmosphere you desire.

➤ **Biophilia Design.**

Biophilia design incorporates elements of nature into the built environment, promoting well-being and reducing stress.

Plants: Incorporate plants into your home office. Plants improve air quality, reduce stress, and create a more calming and inviting atmosphere. Choose plants that are easy to care for and suitable for indoor environments.

➤ **Natural Light and Views**: As mentioned earlier, maximize natural light and views of nature.

➤ **Natural Materials**: Use natural materials, such as wood, stone, and bamboo, in your furniture and decor.

➤ **Nature-Inspired Patterns**: Incorporate nature-inspired patterns and textures into your decor, such as floral prints, wood grain patterns, or natural fiber rugs.

➢ **Water Features**: Consider adding a small water feature, such as a desktop fountain, to create a soothing atmosphere.

❖ **Technology and Productivity**

Technology is an integral part of the modern work-from-home experience. While technology can enhance productivity and efficiency, it can also be a source of distractions and overwhelm. It's essential to use technology effectively, minimize distractions, and create a healthy relationship with digital devices.

❖ **Optimizing Technology for Productivity**

Reliable Internet Connection: A stable internet connection is essential for remote work. Ensure that your internet connection is reliable and that you have an adequate capacity for your work needs.

➢ **Essential Equipment**: Invest in the equipment, such as a computer, monitor, keyboard, mouse, and printer. Choose equipment that is ergonomic and meet your specific work requirements.

➤ **Software and applications**: use software and applications that can enhance your productivity, such as project management tools, communication platforms, and time tracking software.

➤ Organization Systems: Implement digital organization systems to manage your files, emails, and ask effectively. Use folders, labels, and tags to keep your digital space organized.

➤ **Automation Tools:** Explore automation tools that can help you streamline repetitive tasks, such as email filters, calendar reminders, and automated backups.

❖ **Minimizing Digital Distractions**

Digital distractions can significantly affect productivity in the home office. It's important to minimize these distractions and maintain focus.

➤ **Turn Off Notifications:** Disable notifications on your computer, phone, and other devices. Only allow notifications from essential applications or contacts.

- ➢ **Use Website Blockers**: use website blockers or browser extensions to block distracting websites or social media platforms during work hours.
- ➢ **Create Dedicated Work Hours:** Set specific work hours and avoid checking emails or engaging in work-related tasks outside of those hours.
- ➢ **Time Management Techniques**: Implement time management techniques, such as the Pomodoro Technique or time blocking, to stay focused and avoid distractions.
- ➢ **Digital Declutter:** Regularly declutter your digital space by deleting unnecessary files, unsubscribing from unwanted emails, and organizing your digital folders.

❖ **Creating a Healthy Relationship with Digital Devices**

It's important to create a healthy relationship with digital devices and avoid overuse.

- ➢ **Take Breaks from screens:** Take regular breaks from screens throughout the day. Get up, move around, and give your eyes a rest.

- ➢ Limit Screen Time Before Bed: Avoid using screens for at least an hour before bed. The blue light emitted from screens can interfere with sleep.
- ➢ Digital Detox: Consider taking regular digital detoxes, where you disconnect from technology for a period. This can help to reduce stress and improve focus.
- ➢ **Mindful Technology Use:** Be mindful of how you use technology. Avoid mindless scrolling or excessive social media use. Use technology intentionally and purposefully.

❖ **Cybersecurity and Data Protection**

Working from home raises important cybersecurity and data protection considerations.

- ➢ **Secure Your Network**: Ensure that your home Wi-Fi network is secure with a strong password and encryption.
- ➢ **Use a VPN:** Consider using a Virtual Private Network (VPN) to encrypt your internet connection and protect your data.

➢ **Install Antivirus Software**: Install and regularly update antivirus software to protect your devices from malware and viruses.

➢ **Back Up Your Data:** Regularly back up your data to an external drive or cloud storage to prevent data loss.

➢ **Be Cautious of Phishing**: Be cautious of phishing emails or suspicious links. Do not click on links or download attachments from unknown senders.

❖ **Creating a Motivating Environment**

Creating a motivating and inspiring home office environment is essential for maintaining productivity, creativity, and a sense of purpose. Personalizing your space and incorporating elements that reflect your style and interests can help to create a space that you enjoy working in.

❖ **Personalization**

➢ **Reflect Your Style**: Decorate your home office in a way that reflects your personal style. Choose colors, furniture, and decor that you find appealing and inspiring.

- ➤ **Display Meaningful Items**: Display items that are meaningful to you, such as photos, artwork, or souvenirs. These items can serve as reminders of your goals, values, and accomplishments.

- ➤ **Incorporate Hobbies and interests**: Incorporate elements that reflect your hobbies and interests. This could include displaying books, musical instruments, or sports memorabilia.

- ➤ **Create a Vision Board**: Create a vision board with images and words that represent your goals and aspirations. Place it in a prominent location where you can see it regularly.

- ❖ **Fostering Creativity.**

- ➤ **Inspirational Artwork**: Hang artwork that inspires you or stimulates your creativity.

- ➤ **Creative Tools:** Keep creative tools readily available, such as notebooks, pens, drawing supplies, or musical instruments.

- ➤ **Brainstorming Space**: Create a dedicated space for brainstorming, such as a whiteboard, a large notepad, or a comfortable chair with a lap desk.

➤ **Change of Scenery:** Take breaks in an unfamiliar room or go outside for a change of scenery to spark creativity.

❖ **Enhancing Focus.**

➤ **Minimize Clutter**: As discussed throughout this document, minimizing clutter is essential for enhancing focus and reducing distractions.

➤ **Designated Work Area**: Create a designated work area that is separate from other areas of your home. This helps to create a mental distinction between work and personal life.

➤ **Comfortable Seating**: Invest in a comfortable and supportive chair that allows you to sit for extended periods without discomfort.

➤ **Natural Light**: Maximize natural light to improve alertness and focus.

❖ **Maintaining Motivation and Productivity**.

Maintaining motivation and productivity in the home office can be challenging. It's important to establish strategies for overcoming distractions, setting boundaries, and avoiding burnout.

- ➢ **Set Boundaries**: Establish clear boundaries between work and personal life. Set specific work hours and avoid working outside of those hours.

- ➢ **Create a Routine**: Develop a daily routine that includes specific times for work, breaks, and other activities. This helps to create structure and maintain focus.

- ➢ **Take Regular Breaks**: Take regular breaks throughout the day to avoid burnout and maintain focus. Get up, move around, and do something you enjoy.

- ➢ **Avoid Distractions**: Minimize distractions by turning off notifications, using website blockers, and creating a quiet work environment.

- ➢ **Stay Connected:** Stay connected with colleagues, friends, and family. Social interaction can help to boost motivation and prevent feelings of isolation.

- ➢ **Celebrate Successes:** Acknowledge and celebrate your accomplishments, no matter how small. This helps to boost morale and maintain motivation.

- ➢ **Practice Self-Care:** Prioritize self-care activities, such as exercise, healthy eating, and relaxation.

Taking care of yourself physically and mentally is essential for maintaining productivity and well-being.

FINAL THOUGHTS

Optimizing your work-from-home space is a crucial investment in your productivity, well-being, and career success. By applying sound design principles, integrating technology effectively, creating a motivating environment, and cultivating healthy habits, you can transform your home office into a space that supports your goals, inspires your creativity, and empowers you to thrive in the world of remote work. Remember that your work-from-home space should reflect your individual needs, preferences, and aspirations, a place where you can feel comfortable, focused, and motivated to achieve your best.

CHAPTER 9

BALANCING WORK AND HOME ORGANIZATION

Balancing work and home organization requires a strategic approach, especially for those juggling professional responsibilities while maintaining a well-ordered living space. Successfully harmonizing organization in both personal and professional areas reduces stress, enhances efficiency, and frees up more quality time for personal pursuits and family interactions. In today's world, where work and home life often overlap, achieving this balance is essential for overall well-being and productivity.

This chapter explores methods to turn decluttering into a collective effort, making it a shared journey rather than a solo task. It highlights the importance of involving family members or roommates, fostering teamwork, and creating clear roles and responsibilities. We also examine how optimizing shared spaces and integrating consistent organizational habits across both home and work environments can create seamless transitions between professional and personal spheres. By implementing these strategies, individuals can cultivate a culture of order and tranquility that supports both productivity and relaxation.

❖ Coordinating Decluttering Tasks with Family or Roommates

Decluttering as a shared responsibility can be transformative, fostering harmony in both work and home environments. When family members or roommates collaborate on maintaining an organized space, it creates a sense of ownership, teamwork, and accountability.

❖ Setting Collective Goals

Establishing shared goals helps unify efforts and keeps everyone invested in maintaining organization. By agreeing on priorities—such as keeping common areas tidy or ensuring clutter-free kitchen counters—household members develop a mutual commitment to.

Cleanliness. Setting realistic expectations and defining specific objectives encourages a collaborative approach, making decluttering more manageable and effective.

When embarking on a decluttering journey with family or roommates, it's crucial to lay a solid foundation with clearly defined and collectively agreed-upon goals. This process not only aligns everyone's efforts, but also fosters a sense of unity and shared purpose. Begin by initiating an open and inclusive discussion where each member can voice their vision of an organized living space. Encourage the expression of individual priorities, concerns, and ideas, ensuring that everyone feels heard and valued.

Identify specific areas that require attention and discuss the desired outcomes for each. Prioritize spaces that are shared or frequently used, such as the living room, kitchen, or entryway. Establish clear objectives for these areas, such as maintaining clutter-free surfaces, implementing efficient storage solutions, or creating designated zones for specific items.

Involve everyone in the decision-making process, allowing for negotiation and compromise to accommodate diverse needs and preferences. This collaborative approach ensures that the goals are realistic, achievable, and reflective of the collective vision.

Define what a successful outcome looks like for each space. This might involve setting specific standards for cleanliness, organization, or functionality. For example, in the kitchen, the goal might be to have all countertops clear after meals, dishes washed and put away promptly, and pantry items neatly arranged and labeled.

By establishing these shared goals, household members develop a mutual commitment to cleanliness and order. This collective agreement fosters accountability, with everyone invested in upholding standards and maintaining an organized environment.

❖ Organizing Group Cleaning Sessions

Scheduling group decluttering sessions can make the process more engaging and efficient. Turning tidying up into a shared activity—perhaps with a timer or a rewards system—adds an element of fun and motivation. Assigning specific tasks ensures each participant contributes meaningfully. For example, one person might focus on organizing storage spaces while another handles dusting and tidying surfaces.

Encouraging input from everyone fosters a sense of inclusion and creativity in designing storage solutions and optimizing shared areas.

Regular group decluttering sessions turn what might seem a mundane chore into an engaging and efficient activity. By scheduling regular sessions where everyone takes part, you not only expedite the decluttering process but also foster a sense of camaraderie and shared responsibility.

To make these sessions enjoyable and motivating, consider incorporating elements of fun and gamification. Set a timer for each session, creating a sense of urgency and encouraging focused effort. You can even turn it into a friendly competition, where participants race against the clock to complete their assigned tasks.

Implement a rewards system to reward participation and celebrate achievements. This could involve small treats, a movie night, or any activity that the group enjoys together. Recognizing and acknowledging everyone's contributions reinforces positive habits and creates a positive association with decluttering.

Assign specific tasks to each participant, ensuring that everyone has a clear role and contributes meaningfully to the process. Consider individual strengths, preferences, and availability when allocating responsibilities.

For example, we might ask one person to organize storage spaces, another with dusting and tidying surfaces, and another with sorting and discarding unwanted items.

Encourage open communication and collaboration throughout the sessions. Allow for input from everyone, fostering a sense of inclusion and creativity in designing storage solutions and optimizing shared areas. Brainstorm ideas together, share tips and tricks, and work collaboratively to overcome challenges.

These group decluttering sessions not only expedite the process but also provide an opportunity for bonding and connection. As you work together towards a common goal, you strengthen relationships, improve communication, and create a shared sense of accomplishment.

❖ Assigning Clear Roles

Defining responsibilities for decluttering efforts prevents confusion and ensures accountability. Assigning tasks based on individual strengths or preferences enhances efficiency and engagement. Open communication about expectations reinforces the idea that decluttering is a collective effort rather than a burden on one person. By dispersing responsibilities, maintaining order becomes a sustainable habit rather than a sporadic event.

Assigning clear roles and responsibilities is essential for preventing confusion, ensuring accountability, and fostering a sense of shared ownership in the decluttering process. By defining who handles what, you create a structured framework that enhances efficiency and engagement.

Begin by conducting an assessment of individual strengths, preferences, and availability. Consider each person's skills, interests, and time constraints when allocating tasks. For example, someone who enjoys organizing might declutter closets and drawers, while someone who is detail-oriented might handle digital files and paperwork.

Clearly outline the expectations for each role so that everyone understands their responsibilities and standards. Provide specific instructions, guidelines, or checklists to help individuals fulfill their tasks effectively.

Encourage open communication and feedback throughout the process. Create a safe space where individuals feel comfortable expressing concerns, asking questions, or suggesting improvements. Regularly check in with each person to ensure they have the resources and support they need to succeed in their assigned roles.

Reinforce the idea that decluttering is a collective effort, not a burden to be carried by one individual. Emphasize the importance of teamwork, collaboration, and mutual support. Acknowledge and appreciate everyone's contributions, fostering a sense of shared responsibility and accomplishment.

By dispersing responsibilities and fostering open communication, you create a sustainable system where maintaining order becomes a natural part of the household routine. This collaborative approach transforms decluttering from a sporadic event into an ongoing habit, promoting long-term organization and harmony.

❖ **Celebrating Small Wins**

Recognizing progress keeps motivation high and reinforces positive habits. Whether it's clearing out a cluttered closet, maintaining an organized desk, or successfully completing a group cleaning session, acknowledging achievements—through simple rewards like a family dinner or a movie night—encourages continued efforts. Valuing organization creates an environment that facilitates the maintenance of long-term habits. Decluttering as a team strengthens relationships, improves communication, and fosters a shared sense of accomplishment. As tidiness becomes a routine, maintaining an organized home becomes second nature, promoting both mental clarity and a peaceful living environment.

Celebrating small wins powerfully maintains motivation, reinforces positive habits, and creates a culture that values and appreciates the organization.

Recognizing progress, no matter how incremental, provides a sense of accomplishment and encourages continued efforts.

Establish a system for acknowledging and celebrating achievements. This could involve verbal praise, a designated "win jar" where you track accomplishments, or a visual progress chart that highlights completed tasks. Regularly review these achievements as a group, taking time to appreciate the collective effort and the positive impact of decluttering.

Tailor the celebrations to suit the preferences and interests of your household. Simple rewards, such as a special family dinner, a movie night, a game session, or a small treat, can serve as effective incentives. The key is to make the celebrations meaningful and enjoyable for everyone involved.

Let's value and celebrate a well-organized environment. Encourage open communication about progress, challenges, and successes.

Share before-and-after photos, discuss the benefits of decluttering, and acknowledge the positive changes in your living space and overall well-being.

Celebrating small wins fosters a sense of teamwork, strengthens relationships, and promotes a shared sense of accomplishment. As you work together to create and maintain an organized environment, you build stronger connections, improve communication, and cultivate a sense of pride in your collective efforts.

As tidiness becomes a routine and organization becomes a shared value, maintaining an organized home becomes second nature. This creates a positive cycle where decluttering is no longer perceived as a chore but as a lifestyle that promotes mental clarity, reduces stress, and fosters a peaceful living environment.

❖ Using Shared Spaces Effectively

Optimizing shared spaces is essential for maintaining balance between work and home organization. Thoughtful space management enhances efficiency while ensuring comfort and functionality in communal areas.

❖ Defining Functional Zones

Clearly defining areas for work, relaxation, and communal activities prevents clutter and maintain boundaries. Creating designated workstations separate from social or leisure areas minimizes distractions and promotes productivity. Simple solutions, such as using bookshelves or decorative dividers, help delineate spaces without requiring structural changes.

In households where multiple individuals share space, we must define functional zones to prevent clutter, maintain boundaries, and promote a harmonious balance between work, relaxation, and communal activities. By clearly delineating areas for specific, you create a structured environment that enhances efficiency and minimizes distractions.

Begin by assessing the layout of your shared spaces and identifying potential areas for each function.

Consider the natural flow of traffic, the availability of natural light, and the existing furniture and fixtures. Designate specific zones for work, relaxation, social interaction, and storage, ensuring that each area serves its intended purpose effectively.

Create designated workstations that are separate from social or leisure areas. This helps to minimize distractions, promote productivity, and establish clear boundaries between work and personal time. If possible, use separate rooms or corners for workstations. If not, employ creative solutions such as using bookshelves, screens, curtains, or decorative dividers to delineate workspaces within a shared room.

Incorporate smart storage solutions to maximize space efficiency and maintain organization within each functional zone. Use multifunctional furniture, such as storage ottomans, sofa beds, or desks with built-in drawers. Implement shelving units, labeled bins, baskets, and wall-mounted organizers to keep items tidy and easily accessible. Vertical storage solutions, such as tall bookshelves or hanging racks, can help free up floor space and create a more spacious feel.

Clearly label each zone and storage container to reinforce its purpose and encourage everyone to maintain order. Use consistent signage, color-coding, or labeling systems to make it easy for everyone to identify where items belong and where activities should take place.

By defining functional zones and implementing smart storage solutions, you create a structured environment that supports the diverse needs of everyone in the household. This thoughtful space management enhances efficiency, promotes productivity, and fosters a sense of harmony and balance in shared living areas.

❖ Incorporating Smart Storage Solutions

Using multifunctional furniture, such as storage ottomans or foldable desks, maximizes space efficiency. Implementing shelving units, labeled bins, and wall-mounted organizers helps keep shared areas tidy while ensuring accessibility.

Vertical storage solutions, like tall bookshelves or hanging racks, free up floor space and contribute to an uncluttered environment.

In shared living spaces, smart storage solutions are essential for maximizing space efficiency, maintaining organization, and ensuring that everyone's belongings have a designated place. By utilizing innovative storage options, you can create a clutter-free environment that is both functional and aesthetically pleasing.

Multifunctional furniture is a significant change for optimizing space. Consider incorporating items such as storage ottomans, which provide seating while also concealing blankets, pillows, or other items. Sofa beds offer a comfortable seating option that can easily transform into a bed for guests, saving valuable floor space. You can expand foldable desks or tables when needed and then collapse them for storage when not in use, making them ideal for small spaces or flexible work areas.

Shelving units are essential for organizing and displaying items in a tidy and accessible manner. Choose to shelve that complements the style of your shared space and provides ample storage for books, decorative items, and everyday essentials. Customize adjustable shelves to accommodate items of various sizes.

Labeled bins and baskets are invaluable for keeping smaller items organized and contained. Use clear bins to identify contents easily, or choose decorative baskets to add a touch of style to your storage solutions. Label each container clearly to show its contents, making it easy for everyone to find what they need and put items back in their designated place.

Wall-mounted organizers are excellent for maximizing vertical space and keeping surfaces clutter-free.

Install shelves, hooks, racks, or pegboards to store items such as keys, mail, tools, or kitchen utensils. Wall-mounted organizers not only free up valuable counter or floor space but also add a decorative element to your shared areas.

Vertical storage solutions are effective for making the most of limited space. Tall bookshelves, cabinets, or storage units can extend all the way to the ceiling, providing ample storage without taking up valuable floor space.

Hanging racks or shelves can store items such as clothes, towels, or plants, further maximizing vertical space and creating a sense of openness.

By incorporating these smart storage solutions, you can transform shared living spaces into organized, functional, and visually appealing environments where everyone can coexist comfortably and efficiently.

❖ **Implementing Rotational Space Usage**

Flexible use of shared spaces accommodates the varying needs of household members. A dining table might serve as a workstation during work hours and transition back for meals in the evening. Establishing designated time slots for certain spaces ensures fair usage and prevents conflicts, promoting a harmonious living and working environment.

In households with diverse schedules and needs, implementing rotational space usage can be a practical solution for maximizing the functionality of shared areas. This approach involves using spaces for different purposes at different times of the day, ensuring that everyone has access to the resources they need, while minimizing conflicts and promoting a harmonious living environment.

Begin by identifying shared spaces that have the potential for flexible usage. Consider areas like the dining table, living room, or spare bedroom; adapt them to serve multiple functions throughout the day.

Establish a system for scheduling and coordinating the use of these spaces. This could involve creating a shared calendar, using a whiteboard or bulletin board, or using a digital app or platform. Clearly define time slots for specific activities, ensuring that everyone uses the space for their intended purpose.

For example, a dining table might serve as a workstation during work hours, providing a dedicated space for individuals to focus and be productive. In the evening, the same table can transition back to its traditional function, serving as a gathering place for meals and social interaction.

Consider the needs and preferences of each household member when creating the schedule. Consider work schedules, study habits, personal routines, and any other factors that may influence space usage. Be flexible and willing to make adjustments as needed to accommodate changing circumstances.

Establish clear guidelines for transitioning spaces between different functions. This might involve designated storage areas for work-related items, quick cleanup routines, or specific furniture arrangements.

Ensure that everyone understands their responsibilities in maintaining the space and preparing it for its next use.

Communicate regularly and openly about space usage, addressing any concerns or conflicts that may arise. Schedule periodic check-ins to review the effectiveness of the system and make any necessary adjustments. Be willing to compromise and find solutions that work for everyone.

By implementing rotational space usage, you can maximize the functionality of shared areas, accommodate the diverse needs of household members, and create a more efficient and harmonious living and working environment.

❖ Regular Check-Ins for Organization

Periodic discussions about shared space organization encourage feedback and adjustments as needed. Checking in with family members or roommates to assess what's working and what needs improvement ensures that organizational systems remain effective and accommodating for everyone. By optimizing shared areas with practical storage solutions and clearly defined functions, households can maintain organization without sacrificing comfort or flexibility.

Regular check-ins are essential for maintaining effective organization in shared spaces. These periodic discussions provide an opportunity for feedback, address concerns, and ensure that organizational systems remain effective and accommodating for everyone in the household. Schedule regular meetings or informal discussions to review the state of the organization in shared space.

CHAPTER 10

BUILDING A SUPPORTIVE DECLUTTERING COMMUNITY

❖ The Importance of Community in Decluttering

Building a supportive decluttering community can transform personal spaces into havens of tranquility while fostering meaningful connections.

The process of organizing homes and workspaces can sometimes feel overwhelming, especially for busy professionals and work-from-home individuals juggling multiple responsibilities. However, being part of a network of like-minded individuals offers encouragement, accountability, and fresh ideas, making the journey both enjoyable and rewarding. Whether through online groups or local gatherings, these communities provide platforms to share insights, celebrate milestones, and navigate challenges together.

By engaging with others who share similar goals, individuals can gain valuable perspectives and sustain motivation in their decluttering efforts. This chapter explores how to join and build decluttering communities that align with personal goals and lifestyles. We delve into the benefits of participating in online networks, where members can exchange strategies and success stories from around the world.

We highlight the advantages of in-person interactions, where local groups provide face-to-face support and stronger community ties. By leveraging these resources, individuals can stay motivated, learn diverse decluttering techniques, and create spaces that promote balance and productivity.

❖ Joining Online Decluttering Communities

Maintaining an organized living space can be challenging, but community support makes it easier.

Engaging with a network of like-minded individuals fosters accountability and motivation while providing valuable insights into the decluttering process.

❖ Exploring Online Platforms

Online communities provide a convenient way to connect with individuals pursuing similar decluttering goals.

These platforms allow members to exchange ideas, share experiences, and learn from each other's successes and setbacks. Facebook groups, Reddit forums, and specialized websites such as "Declutter My Life" offer extensive resources and discussions on minimalism and organization.

Members gain access to diverse strategies, whether it's tackling sentimental clutter, adopting sustainable decluttering methods, or implementing daily habits to maintain an organized space. Social media also plays a crucial role in fostering engagement.

Platforms like Instagram and Pinterest offer visual inspiration through before-and-after photos, while YouTube provides in-depth tutorials on organization techniques. Hashtags like #DeclutterChallenge or #MinimalismJourney connect users with a global audience, reinforcing motivation and accountability.

By actively taking part in these discussions, individuals can stay inspired and receive real-time feedback on their progress.

❖ **Benefits of Online Communities**

➢ **Accessibility and convenience**: Online groups are accessible anytime, anywhere, making it easy to connect with others regardless of location or schedule. This is beneficial for busy professionals or those with limited mobility.

➢ **Diversity of Perspectives**: Online platforms host a wide range of individuals with different backgrounds, experiences, and decluttering approaches. This diversity allows members to learn about various techniques and find strategies that best suit their needs.

➢ **Anonymity and Comfort:** Some individuals may feel more comfortable sharing their struggles and seeking advice in an online setting, where they can maintain anonymity. This can encourage open and honest discussions.

➢ **East Resources:** Online communities often provide access to a wealth of resources, including articles, blog posts, videos, checklists, and recommended products. Members can tap into this knowledge base to enhance their decluttering efforts.

➤ **24/7 Support:** Online groups are active around the clock, ensuring that members can find support and encouragement whenever they need it. This constant availability can be invaluable during challenging moments in the decluttering process.

❖ **Choosing the Right Online Community**

➤ **Identify Your Goals**: Determine your specific decluttering goals. Are you focused on minimalism, digital decluttering, or organizing a specific space? Look for communities that align with your interests.

➤ **Read the Guidelines:** Familiarize yourself with the group's rules and guidelines to ensure it's a good fit. Some groups may have specific focuses or a particular tone.

➤ **Observe Interactions**: Spend some time observing the interactions within the group. Is it a supportive and positive environment? Do members offer helpful advice and encouragement?

- ➤ **Engage Gradually**: Start by participating in discussions, asking questions, and sharing your own experiences. Build connections with other members.
- ➤ **Use Different Platforms**: Don't limit yourself to just one platform. Explore Facebook groups, Reddit forums, online websites, and social media hashtags to find a variety of communities that resonate with you.

❖ **Taking part in Local Decluttering Groups**

While online groups offer accessibility and a wealth of ideas, in-person interactions provide deeper connections and immediate support.

Local decluttering groups or workshops encourage hands-on collaboration, allowing members to work together on shared goals.

These gatherings create opportunities for structured decluttering sessions, skill-sharing, and even item exchanges to help reduce waste and repurpose belongings.

Joining or forming a local decluttering club can lead to monthly meetups where participants discuss challenges, share organizing techniques, and celebrate progress.

These interactions not only enhance decluttering efforts but also build lasting friendships and a sense of community.

Attending workshops, organizing group decluttering projects, or taking part in community clean-up events can further strengthen these connections and make the process more fulfilling.

❖ **Benefits of Local Communities**

➢ **Face-to-Face Interaction**: In-person meetings allow for more personal connections and stronger community ties. This can lead to deeper relationships and a greater sense of belonging.

➢ **Hands-on Support**: Local groups can offer practical, hands-on help with decluttering projects. Members might help each other sort through belongings, organize spaces, or transport items for donation.

➢ **Skill-Sharing and Workshops**: Local groups often organize workshops and skill-sharing sessions where members can learn new decluttering techniques, DIY organization projects, or upcycling methods.

➢ **Accountability and Motivation**: Meeting regularly with a local group can provide a strong sense of accountability and motivation. Members can set goals together, track progress, and encourage each other to stay on track.

➢ **Community Engagement**: Local groups can take part in community events, such as organizing donation drives, hosting swap meets, or volunteering for neighborhood clean-ups. This fosters a sense of purpose and contributes to the well-being of the wider community.

❖ **Finding Local Decluttering Groups**

➢ **Check Community Centers**: Community centers, libraries, and local organizations often host workshops, classes, or support groups related to decluttering and organization.

➢ **Search Online Directories**: Websites and online directories may list local groups or clubs in your area. Use keywords such as "decluttering group," "organizing club," or "minimalism meetup" along with your city or town.

➢ **Use Social media**. Social media platforms can be a valuable tool for finding local groups. Search for relevant groups on Facebook, Meetup, or other platforms.

➢ **Ask at Local Businesses**: Some local businesses, such as organizing stores or consignment shops, may know or host decluttering groups or events.

➢ **Start Your Own Group**: If you can't find an existing group, consider starting your own! Reach out to friends, neighbors, or colleagues who might be interested in decluttering and organize an initial meeting.

❖ **Organizing Effective Local Meetups**

➢ **Choose a Convenient Location**: Select a location that is easily accessible for most members, such as a community center, library, or local coffee shop.

- ➤ **Set a Regular Schedule**: Establish a regular meeting schedule, such as monthly or bi-weekly, to ensure consistency and allow members to plan.

- ➤ **Plan Engaging Activities**: Vary the activities at each meetup to keep things interesting. This might include discussions, skill-sharing sessions, decluttering challenges, or group outings.

- ➤ **Create a Welcoming Atmosphere**: Foster a supportive and inclusive environment where everyone feels comfortable sharing their experiences and seeking advice.

- ➤ **Use Technology:** Use email or social media to communicate with members, share resources, and organize events.

❖ **Combining Online and Local Support**

Finding the Right Fit

Every individual has different decluttering needs, making it essential to find a group that aligns with personal goals and lifestyle.

Some may prefer niche communities focusing on downsizing, while others may benefit from general organization groups.

Exploring various options—both online and in person—ensures exposure to different methodologies and approaches.

Learning about cultural perspectives on minimalism, such as Japanese or Scandinavian design principles, can introduce fresh decluttering philosophies that resonate on a personal level.

By engaging in diverse decluttering communities, individuals can gain new insights, build accountability, and maintain long-term success in their organizing efforts.

❖ **Synergistic Benefits**

Combining online and local decluttering communities can provide a synergistic effect, offering the benefits of both types of support systems.

➤ **Broadened Network:** taking part in both online and local groups expands your network of decluttering enthusiasts, increasing your exposure to diverse perspectives and resources.

➢ **Enhanced Motivation:** The combination of online and in-person support can provide a powerful boost to motivation. Online communities offer constant encouragement and inspiration, while local groups provide accountability and hands-on help.

➢ **Practical Application:** Online communities can provide theoretical knowledge and inspiration, while local groups offer opportunities to apply those concepts in a practical setting, such as through group decluttering projects or skill-sharing workshops.

➢ Stronger Sense of Community: taking part in both types of communities can foster a stronger sense of belonging and connection. Online groups provide a global network of support, while local groups offer a more intimate and localized community.

➢ **Flexibility and adaptability**: Combining online and local support allows for greater flexibility and adaptability. You can engage with online communities whenever it's convenient for you, while local groups provide opportunities for in-person interaction and support when you need it.

❖ **Strategies for Integration**

➢ **Share Online Resources Locally**: Share helpful articles, videos, or websites from online communities with your local group members. This can introduce them to new ideas and resources.

➢ **Organize Local Meetups for Online Groups**: If you're active in an online decluttering group, consider organizing local meetups for members in your area. This can provide an opportunity to connect in person and build stronger relationships.

➢ **Use Online Platforms to Promote Local Events**: Use online platforms to promote local decluttering events, workshops, or group meetups. This can help attract more participants and expand your local community.

➢ **Create Hybrid Events:** Consider organizing hybrid events that combine online and in-person elements. For example, you could host a decluttering workshop that is streamed online for those who can't attend in person.

➢ **Foster Communication Between Groups**: Encourage communication and collaboration between online and local groups. This could involve cross-promoting events, sharing resources, or organizing joint projects.

❖ **Sharing and Exchanging Decluttering Success Stories**

Sharing personal experiences fosters deeper connections and provides valuable lessons for others on the same journey.

Whether through storytelling, social media, or journaling, exchanging success stories creates a sense of community and encouragement.

❖ **Storytelling as a Motivational Tool**

Personal stories offer inspiration by showcasing real-life challenges and triumphs.

Whether discussing the emotional difficulty of parting with sentimental items or the relief of achieving an organized home, storytelling resonates with others facing similar struggles.

Engaging in group discussions, blog writing, or podcast interviews allows individuals to share insights and encourage others to continue their decluttering journeys.

❖ **The Power of Narrative.**

➢ **Emotional Connection:** Stories have the power to evoke emotions and create a sense of connection between individuals. Sharing your personal decluttering story can help others feel understood and less alone in their struggles.

➢ **Inspiration and Motivation**: Success stories can be incredibly inspiring and motivating. Hearing about someone else's journey and how they overcame challenges can give others the confidence and encouragement to pursue their own decluttering goals.

➢ **Learning from Others:** Stories often contain valuable lessons and insights. By sharing your experiences, you can help others learn from your mistakes, adopt effective strategies, and avoid common pitfalls.

➤ **Building Empathy**: Sharing your story can help build empathy and understanding within a decluttering community. It allows others to see the human side of decluttering and appreciate the emotional and psychological aspects of the process.

➤ **Creating a Sense of Community**: Sharing stories foster a sense of community and belonging. It creates a space where individuals feel comfortable sharing their vulnerabilities, celebrating their successes, and supporting each other through challenges.

❖ **Platforms for Sharing Stories**

➤ **Group Discussions**: Local decluttering groups provide a natural setting for sharing stories and experiences. During meetings or workshops, members can take turns sharing their successes, challenges, and insights.

➤ **Online Forums and Communities**: Online platforms offer a wide audience for sharing decluttering stories. Members can post their stories in forums, discussion boards, or social media groups.

- ➤ **Blogs and Websites**: Creating a blog or website can provide a dedicated space for sharing your decluttering journey. You can write about your experiences, share tips and advice, and connect with others who are interested in decluttering.

- ➤ **Podcasts and Videos:** Podcasts and videos offer a dynamic way to share your decluttering story. You can record interviews, create tutorials, or document your progress through vlogs.

- ➤ **Workshops and Presentations**: If you have a passion for decluttering, consider sharing your story through workshops or presentations. This can be a great way to inspire and educate others.

- ❖ **Tips for Effective Storytelling**

- ➤ **Be Authentic**: Share your genuine experiences, both the difficulties. Authenticity resonates with others and creates a stronger connection.

- ➤ **Focus on the Emotional Journey**: Decluttering is often an emotional process. Share your feelings, thoughts, and challenges to help others understand the deeper aspects of decluttering.

- ➤ **Highlight Key Lessons**: Emphasize the key lessons you learned along the way. What advice would you give to someone who is just starting their decluttering journey?
- ➤ **Use Visuals:** If possible, use visuals to enhance your storytelling. Before-and-after photos, videos, or diagrams can help illustrate your progress and inspire others.
- ➤ **Engage with Your Audience:** Respond to comments, questions, and feedback. Engage in discussions and build relationships with those who are interested in your story.

❖ **Using Social Media for Engagement**

Blogging and social media platforms provide a powerful medium for documenting decluttering progress and inspiring others.

Instagram, YouTube, and TikTok allow individuals to showcase before-and-after transformations, discuss organizational techniques, and engage with a wider audience.

Creating a posting schedule and responding to comments fosters a sense of connection and accountability within the community.

❖ **Choosing the Right Platforms**

➤ **Instagram:** Instagram is a visually driven platform that is ideal for sharing before-and-after photos, creating aesthetically pleasing layouts, and using relevant hashtags to reach a wider audience.

➤ **YouTube:** YouTube is a video-sharing platform that allows you to create in-depth tutorials, document your decluttering journey through vlogs, or share interviews with other decluttering enthusiasts.

➤ **TikTok:** TikTok is a short-form video platform that is popular for creating engaging and entertaining decluttering content, such as quick tips, time-lapse transformations, or humorous skits.

➤ **Facebook:** Facebook is a versatile platform that can create groups, share posts, host live sessions, and connect with a local or global decluttering community.

➢ **Pinterest:** Pinterest is a visual discovery platform that is ideal for curating inspiration boards, sharing organizing ideas, and driving traffic to your decluttering blog or website.

❖ **Creating Engaging Content**

➢ **High-Quality Visuals**: Use clear, well-lit photos and videos that showcase your decluttering progress. Pay attention to composition, lighting, and editing to create visually appealing content.

➢ **Variety of Content**: Mix up your content to keep your audience engaged. Share before-and-after photos, decluttering tips, organizational hacks, personal stories, and behind-the-scenes glimpses into your journey.

➢ **Authenticity and Transparency:** Be genuine in your content. Share your struggles, challenges, and setbacks, along with your successes. Authenticity builds trust and connection with your audience.

➢ **Educational and Informative Content**: Provide valuable information and insights that can help others on their decluttering journey. Share practical tips, research-backed advice, and personal experiences that can empower your audience.

➤ **Interactive Content**: Encourage engagement by asking questions, hosting polls, running contests, or creating challenges. Respond to comments and messages to foster a sense of community and connection.

❖ **Building a Posting Schedule**

➤ **Consistency is Key**: Develop a consistent posting schedule to keep your audience engaged and coming back for more. Determine how often you can realistically post and stick to that schedule as much as possible.

➤ **Plan Your Content**: Create a content calendar to plan your posts in advance. This will help you stay organized, ensure a variety of content, and avoid last-minute scrambling for ideas.

➤ **Use Scheduling Tools**: use social media scheduling tools to automate your posts and save time. These tools let you schedule posts in advance for optimal publication times.

➢ **Analyze Your Analytics**: Pay attention to your social media analytics to see what type of content performs best and when your audience is most active. Use this data to refine your posting schedule and content strategy.

➢ **Engage with Your Audience:** Don't just post and forget. Take the time to respond to comments, messages, and questions from your audience. Engage in conversations, build relationships, and foster a sense of community.

❖ **Journaling for Self-Reflection**

Journaling serves as a personal tool for tracking decluttering progress, setting goals, and reflecting on emotional attachments to possessions.

Writing accomplishments and challenges helps individuals stay mindful of their journey and recognize patterns that influence their habits.

Establishing a regular journaling practice—such as recording daily or weekly reflections—enhances self-awareness and reinforces positive decluttering behaviors.

CONCLUSION

In today's fast-paced world, balancing demanding careers and home lives often means that maintaining an organized space takes a backseat. Yet, creating harmony in our living and working environments is essential for achieving balance, reducing stress, and enhancing productivity. By embracing the philosophy of decluttering, busy professionals and work-from-home individuals can unlock benefits that extend beyond mere organization—it is a transformative process that nurtures both physical and mental well-being.

Decluttering is not just about eliminating excess; it is about curating an environment that fosters clarity, focus, and tranquility. Each decluttered space—whether a desk, a room, or an entire home—becomes a reflection of intentionality, breathing new life into daily routines. With an organized space, concentration improves, creativity flourishes, and stress diminishes, creating an atmosphere that supports both professional success and personal fulfillment.

The foundation of successful decluttering lies in setting realistic and achievable goals. The thought of a complete home overhaul can feel overwhelming, but breaking the process down into small, manageable tasks makes it more attainable. Each milestone reached— whether clearing out a single drawer or reorganizing a workspace—fuels motivation and transforms decluttering into an empowering journey rather than a daunting chore. Celebrating these incremental successes reinforces progress and fosters long-term commitment.

Equally important is the power of community support. Just as teamwork is invaluable in professional settings, engaging with a supportive network can make decluttering a more enjoyable and sustainable process. Sharing experiences, strategies, and insights with like-minded individuals fosters accountability, inspiration, and encouragement.

Whether through online forums, social media groups, or in-person meetups, connecting with a decluttering community transforms what might have been a solitary task into a collaborative and enriching experience.

Flexibility and adaptability are also key elements in sustaining long-term decluttering success. Life is unpredictable, and rigid approaches can lead to frustration. Recognizing the need to adjust strategies as circumstances develop ensures that decluttering remains a sustainable practice rather than a temporary fix. By maintaining a flexible mindset, individuals can integrate organization into their daily routines in a way that aligns with their lifestyle and responsibilities.

Ultimately, decluttering is a deeply personal journey. There is no universal blueprint—each individual must tailor their approach to suit their unique needs and aspirations. It is not about achieving perfection but about creating an environment that enhances well-being, efficiency, and peace of mind. Every decision to keep or let go of an item should reflect a conscious effort toward simplifying and improving one's life.

For those balancing professional ambitions with the desire for a serene and efficient home, decluttering offers invaluable lessons. It teaches the art of prioritization, the beauty of simplicity, and the undeniable impact that an organized environment has on mental clarity and productivity. Decluttering is not just about tidying up—it is an ongoing practice of redefining one's relationship with space, cultivating a lifestyle where functionality meets inspiration.

As you embark on your own decluttering journey, embrace the process with curiosity, patience, and commitment. Stay connected to your goals, seek support when needed, and remain adaptable in your approach. Each small step contributes to a larger transformation, leading to a life filled with greater clarity, intention, and satisfaction.

By choosing to declutter, you are making an investment in your future—a future characterized by efficiency, productivity, and joy. This journey is about more than reorganizing physical items; it is about reshaping your life, one mindful decision at a time. Move forward with purpose, let your surroundings reflect your aspirations, and create a space that empowers you to thrive both personally and professionally. The journey may have its challenges, but the rewards—greater peace, enhanced focus, and a harmonious balance between home and work—are immeasurable.

REFERENCE

Chapter 1

- Blocked. (2025). *The powerful connection between decluttering and speeding up personal growth.* Thejaychase.com. https://thejaychase.com/blogs/news/spark-joy-spark-success-the-powerful-connection-between-decluttering-and-accelerating-personal-growth

- Itsmynest.com. (2025). *Minimalists and decluttering.* https://itsmynest.com/minimalists-decluttering/

- TJ, T. J. (2024, November 26). *Before You Build Your Personal Knowledge Management System, Read This First.* Medium. https://medium.com/@theo-james/before-you-build-your-personal-knowledge-management-system-read this-first-051cb584b3b4

- The. (2024, July 27). *Psychology of clutter: A storage unit perspective.* Rock Solid Storage. https://www.rocksolidstorage.net/blog/psychology-of-clutter-storage-unit-perspective

- *The Ultimate Guide To Organizing And Decluttering Your Home.* (2024, April 19). Thacleaning.com. https://www.thacleaning.com/ultimate-guide-to-organizing-decluttering-home/

172

- Miss Organized. (2023, July 31). *Professional Organizing Services in San Diego - Miss Organized.* https://missorganized.com/miss-organized-organizing-podcast/

- Jain, V. K., Gupta, A., & Verma, H. (2023, June 8). *Goodbye materialism: Exploring antecedents of minimalism and its impact on millennials' well-being.* Environment, Development and Sustainability. https://doi.org/10.1007/s10668-023-03437-0

- Momorie. (2025, January 9). *Why is decluttering important? 2025 real user experience.* Lemon8. https://www.lemon8-app.com/experience/the-importance-of-decluttering-your-space?region=sg

Chapter 2

- Beyond BookSmart. (2024, November 5). What Are Ruminating Thoughts and How Can You Stop Them? Beyondbooksmart.com; Beyond BookSmart. https://doi.org/10558196/module_165612562967_header-global-moduleV2

- Find Michele Delory's tips on organizing, minimalist living and the Komari Method. (2024). MODERN & MINIMALIST. https://www.modernandminimalist.com/blog.html

- Gumnick, E. F. (2025, January 17). Survey #242 Results: Decluttering and Organizing Mindset Pre-test. The Clutter Fairy. https://www.clutterfairyhouston.com/survey-242-results-decluttering-and-organizing-mindset-pre-test/

- Hive, M. @ O. H. (2023, December 21). Simplify Your Life: Declutter your Schedule. Our Happy Hive. https://ourhappyhive.com/simplify-your-life-declutter-your-schedule/

- Melissa. (2014, December 31). A Bag A Day Keeps The Clutter Away {12 Months of Decluttering} - The Inspired Room. The Inspired Room. https://theinspiredroom.net/a-bag-a-day-keeps-the-clutter-away-twelve-month-decluttering/

- Qusay Alzubaidy. (2024, July 22). 5 Productivity Hacks - Daily Wavelength - Medium. Medium; Daily Wavelength. https://medium.com/daily-wavelength/5-productivity-hacks-9423a06970eb

Chapter 3

- Arevalo, J. (2022, April 15). Choose Your 15 Minutes a Day | The Organized Military Life. The Organized Military Life. https://theorganizedmilitarylife.com/choose-your-15-minutes-a-day/

- Celeste. (2018, June 6). The 15 Minute Daily Cleaning Routine Your Home is Begging For | Decor by the Seashore. Decor by the Seashore. https://decorbytheseashore.com/15-minute-daily-cleaning-routine/

- Godreau, J. (2024, March 22). Declutter Your Home, Declutter Your Mind: The Path to Mental Clarity. Mindful Health Solutions. https://mindfulhealthsolutions.com/declutter-your-home-declutter-your-mind-the-path-to-mental-clarity/

- Jones, R. (2015, May 26). The Clutter-Depression-Anxiety Cycle: How to Stop It. Nourishing Minimalism. https://nourishingminimalism.com/clutter-depression-and-anxiety-a-vicious-cycle/

- Poplin, J. (2024, November 23). The 2-Minute Decluttering Rule: 5 Ways This Small Effort Makes a Big Difference - The Simplicity Habit. The Simplicity Habit. https://www.thesimplicityhabit.com/2-minute-decluttering-rule/

- Quintana, D. (2024, June 9). Small Tasks, Big Rewards: The Benefits Of Doing Small Tasks Immediately. Medium; Medium. https://dnqsolutions.medium.com/small-tasks-big-rewards-the-benefits-of-doing-small-tasks-immediately-2725903e7cbb

Chapter 4

- Atomic DC. (2023, March 28). Savvy Organizing Tools for Busy Professionals | Sorted Out. Sorted out Professional Organizers.

https://www.sortedout.com/savvy-organizing-tools-for-busy-professionals/

- GGI Insights. (2023, September 11). How to Declutter Fast: The 24-Hour Challenge. Graygroupintl.com; Gray Group International LLC. https://www.graygroupintl.com/blog/how-to-declutter-fast

- Simplicity, B. T. (2021, October 18). Minimalism and Time Management: How The Minimalist Lifestyle Can Improve Your Productivity. BALANCE through SIMPLICITY. https://balancethroughsimplicity.com/how-minimalism-improves-time-management-and-productivity/

- Schahaff, K. (2024, January 16). "Unleash Your Radiance: The Art of Life Liberation through Decluttering." Keisha Schahaff. https://www.keishaschahaff.com/post/unleash-your-radiance-the-art-of-life-liberation-through-decluttering

- The Many Mental Benefits of Decluttering | Psychology Today. (n.d.). Www.psychologytoday.com. https://www.psychologytoday.com/us/blog/the-resilient-brain/202302/the-many-mental-benefits-of-decluttering

- \r\n \n Decluttering for Greater Productivity\n \r\n. (2022). Mercerislandchamber.com.

https://www.mercerislandchamber.com/declutterin
g-for-greater-productivity

Chapter 5

- 5 Steps to Keeping a Clean and Organized Office. (n.d.). Business.com. https://www.business.com/articles/organize-your-workspace/

- Hayley. (2023, July 21). Clutter and Mental Health: The Psychological Impact of a Disorganized Space. Simple Joy. https://simplejoy.co.uk/2023/07/21/clutter-and-mental-health/

- Lail, K. (2024, March 6). The Power of a Clean Desk: Boosting Productivity and Efficiency in the Workplace. IdealTraits. https://idealtraits.com/blog/the-power-of-a-clean-desk-boosting-productivity-and-efficiency-in-the-workplace/

- News, N. (2023, September 4). Why Household Mess Triggers Stress and Anxiety. Neuroscience News. https://neurosciencenews.com/anxiety-stress-messy-home-23874/

- Sander, L. (2019, January 25). What does clutter do to your brain and body? NewsGP. https://www1.racgp.org.au/newsgp/clinical/what-does-clutter-do-to-your-brain-and-body

- Thompson, S. (2025). The Science of Decluttering: How Document Organization Boosts Mental Clarity | Ahead App Blog. Ahead-App.com. https://ahead-app.com/blog/procrastination/the-science-of-decluttering-how-document-organization-boosts-mental-clarity-20250117-033234

Chapter 6

- Brinson, M. J. (2023, August 28). Finding Freedom from Clutter: Overcoming Emotional Attachments and Resistance. The Relationship Center. https://www.therelationshipcentre.ca/finding-freedom-from-clutter-overcoming-emotional-attachments-and-resistance/

- Decluttering: The Untold Impact on Well-Being and Productivity. (n.d.). Www.graygroupintl.com. https://www.graygroupintl.com/blog/decluttering

- Declutterbuzz. (2023, June 30). The Art Of Minimalism And Living With Intention - Declutter buzz - Medium. Medium. https://medium.com/@declutterbuzz/the-art-of-minimalism-and-living-with-intention-e57cbd0eca85

- How. (2023, September 18). Interior Design in Seattle & Bellevue | Elegant Simplicity. Interior Design in Seattle & Bellevue | Elegant Simplicity. https://elegantsi.com/blog/sentimental-clutter

- Knyszewski, J. (2024, August 12). Embracing Minimalism: How Simplifying Your Life Can Lead to Greater Happiness and Efficiency. Medium; Medium. https://medium.com/@thejeromeknyszewski/embracing-minimalism-how-simplifying-your-life-can-lead-to-greater-happiness-and-efficiency-ea16d90e7c97

- The Mental Health Benefits of Minimalism. (2024). Grandrisingbehavioralhealth.com. https://www.grandrisingbehavioralhealth.com/blog/the-mental-health-benefits-of-minimalism

Chapter 7

- Burner, S. (2023, October 16). How to Be More Organized at Work? 15 Strategies & Templates. ClickUp. https://clickup.com/blog/how-to-be-more-organized-at-work/

- Hill, J. (2016, December 20). The Advantages of Designates Warehouse Spaces. RMH Systems. https://www.rmhsystems.com/the-benefits-of-designated-spaces-in-your-warehouse/

- O'Connor, E. (2023, October 13). Self Accountability: 10 Ways To Do It Properly. Dr. Eddie O'Connor. https://dreddieoconnor.com/blog/self-accountability/

- The Secret to Reducing Clutter and Improving Operational Flow - Facilities Management Advisor. (2024, October 4). Facilities Management Advisor. https://facilitiesmanagementadvisor.blr.com/maintenance-and-operations/the-secret-to-reducing-clutter-and-improving-operational-flow/

- https://www.facebook.com/AndreaDekkerDOTcom. (2019, March 29). My Year-Round Approach to Home Management. Andrea Dekker. https://andreadekker.com/year-round-home-management/

- webbercookn. (2024, October 29). Creating a Monthly Motivation Plan for Your Goals - webbercookn - Medium. Medium. https://webbercookn.medium.com/creating-a-monthly-motivation-plan-for-your-goals-a3a8c77c56f5

Chapter 8

- Cyber Vintage. (2025). Cyber Vintage. https://cyber-vintage.com/blogs/desk-setups/what-are-the-benefits-of-a-personalized-desk-setup?srsltid=AfmBOoptY3JySdHh-iSzCHbTQh3eWmgo2PQwN5ikt5O2KTf9rSqIr6t-

- Ergonomic Workstation Benefits. (2025). Aceofficesystems.com. https://aceofficesystems.com/blogs/news/ergonomic-workstation-benefits

- G, B. (2024, July 4). Patriot Maids. Patriot Maids. https://patriotmaids.com/boston-services/professional-organizers/digital-organization-made-easy/

- Illumtori. (2024, January 11). Streamlining Your Digital Workspace for Peak Productivity. Medium. https://medium.com/@illumtori/streamlining-your-digital-workspace-for-peak-productivity-7700912876a6

- Mayo Clinic. (2023, May 25). Office ergonomics: Your how-to guide. Mayo Clinic. https://www.mayoclinic.org/healthy-lifestyle/adult-health/in-depth/office-ergonomics/art-20046169

- Saffron Marigold. (2022, August 13). How to Create an Inspiring Workspace: 11 Artistic Tips - Saffron Marigold. Saffron Marigold. https://www.saffronmarigold.com/blog/how-to-create-an-inspiring-workspace/?srsltid=AfmBOoqAgeT3ZQ4hOkvk-LVzrER-cQY8NO-R9qfza-r_cETJ1PGL7zXH

Chapter 9

- Downsizing Decluttering. (2023, October 31). 3 Creative Ways to Deal with "Other People's Clutter" | Design Services LTD. Design Services LTD | Rita Wilkins, the Downsizing Designer, is a Nationally Recognized Interior Design and Lifestyle Design Expert. Through Her Best-Selling Book, Speaking engagements, and Design Insight,

181

Rita Has Changed the Lives of Thousands of People throughout the United States. https://www.designservicesltd.com/2023/10/31/3-creative-ways-to-deal-with-other-peoples-clutter/

- Inc, G. M. (2023, June 4). The Power of Routine: Establishing Consistent Cleaning Habits for a Clutter-Free Life. Golden Maid Inc. https://goldenmaidservices.com/the-power-of-routine-establishing-consistent-cleaning-habits-for-a-clutter-free-life/

- Mastering task management: Your invisible productivity superpower | Align: The Time Blocking App. (2023). Align: The Time Blocking App. https://align.day/blog/task-management/

- Neves, J. (2022, May 3). Task Management: How To Stay Organized And Productive. Day.io. https://day.io/blog/task-management-how-to-stay-organized-and-productive/

- Small, M. (2024, November 20). Lord Decor. Lord Decor. https://www.lorddecor.com/blog/maximizing-small-shared-office-spaces-creative-layout-ideas

- Wanichko, N. (n.d.). Maximize Your Shared Office Space with these 5 Tips! Www.yarooms.com. https://www.yarooms.com/blog/5-ideas-to-optimize-your-shared-office-space

Chapter 10

- Boris, V. (2017). What Makes Storytelling So Effective For Learning? Harvard Business Publishing. https://www.harvardbusiness.org/what-makes-storytelling-so-effective-for-learning/

- Boston University. (n.d.). The Power of Storytelling to Facilitate Human Connection and Learning | affect. Sites.bu.edu. https://sites.bu.edu/impact/previous-issues/impact-summer-2022/the-power-of-storytelling/

- Dynys, J. (2023, November 7). Decluttering Motivation | A Comprehensive Guide to Decluttering Your Home. The Everyday Farmhouse. https://theeverydayfarmhouse.com/decluttering-motivation/

- Gabriel-Pollock, M. (2023, November 15). Simplify Experts. Simplify Experts. https://simplifyexperts.com/give-away-your-stuff-online/

- Organized, S. (2021, May 24). Oh, So Organized. Oh, so organized. https://www.ohsoorganized.com/blog/motivation-to-declutter

- Trumpbour, S. (2024, April 17). Upcycling Your Clutter - Connect to Northern Westchester. Connect to Northern Westchester - We Tell

Engaging Stories That Connect Our Readers to the People and Businesses That Comprise Our Beautiful Community.
https://connecttomag.com/upcycling-your-clutter/

Printed in Dunstable, United Kingdom

65104109R00109